The Magic-System Blueprint

By C. R. Rowenson

The Magic-System Blueprint

First Edition

By C. R. Rowenson

Editor: Little Guy Editing

ISBN: 978-1-7379773-0-8 (pbk)

ISBN: 978-1-7379773-1-5 (hbk)

ISBN: 978-1-7379773-2-2 (ebook)

Acknowledgements

To My Friends and Family
You know who you are.

You all get to see me at my best and my worst, and yet you're always there supporting me, encouraging me, and helping me stabilize myself mentally and emotionally. I couldn't be more thankful for having you in my life.

Alpha and Beta Readers
Abbey Atkinson, Alex Bird Tilson, April Haman, Austin Alander, Christian Casey, Daniel Eavenson, Helen P. Stavropoulos Sandoval, Ian Woodworth, Leah Birgquist, Lionel Sondey, Syeda Hadia Abbas, and Torie Fox.

You all looked past the quirks and faults to see the book as it could be, and then you helped me get it there. I hope you enjoyed the journey as much as I did.

To My Indiegogo Backers
Abbey Atkinson, Amanda Taylor, B.C. Krygowski, Carrie Defever, Catherine Kissner, Chautona Havig, Cheryl Whitmore, Chris Rickard, Chris Thomas, C.A. Pence, Courtney Staples, Daniel Eavenson, Danny Mandel, Daniel Quinn, Dante Morales, David Balsiger, David Langlois, David Martinez, Elli Comeau, Filip Thorén, Gretchen Hefley, Helen Stavropoulos Sandoval, House Alekseii, Ian Woodworth, Caleb Huitt, Jacob Hawes, Jessica Moss, Jonathan Mathurin, Kat Klettke, Keith McCormick, Kent Laue, Larissa Soehn, Laura Blegen, Laura Lützen, Laura Lundy, Lupus590, Nikki Tuberty, Onnonomad, Osmo Korhonen, Peter Chiykowski, Rachel Jones, Rachel Moore, Robyn Schwartz, Rebekka Allgayer, Rob Hilferty, Robert Connick, Robert Zsolt Nagy, Roland Denzel, Rowan North, Sara Becker, Terry Mixon, Thomas Larsen, Tracywc, Tyree R. Middleton, Victoria Meredith, Wilbur Ralston, William Dew, and William Jinkins

I wasn't sure how this book would be received or if there would be much interest at all. Well, here you are to silence my inner pessimist. You have my honest, heartfelt thanks for your support and encouragement.

Contents

The Magic-System Blueprint

PART ONE

Introduction

W ELCOME TO *The Magic-System Blueprint*. The Blueprint is a magic-building tool designed to quickly give you a holistic understanding of any magic system. This book will introduce you to the tool, map out several popular magic systems, and provide detailed information on all the tool's components.

This book has been a long time in the making. It's been over a decade since I first realized how little information there was on magic-building. Plenty of magic-builders, blog posts, and videos exist, but they all seem to ask the same open-ended questions and provide the same general guidelines. Magic-building was, and is, mostly treated as an art form without clear guidance or analysis.

So I explored how different people designed them, dissected why they work, developed theories, formed structures, and crafted tools to simplify the process and communicate my findings with other authors.

Ten years later, here we are, with the first robust, defined, and tested magic-building tool: *The Magic-System Blueprint*.

This tool exists to help you differentiate the fundamental aspects of various magic systems so you can crack open any system and identify the moving parts that make it work. It also provides a framework to quickly map out your own magic systems while ensuring no key elements have been missed.

Before I say anything else, I want to make something abundantly clear. If something in this book doesn't work for you, don't use it!

The Magic-System Blueprint isn't the only way to build or understand magic systems; it is simply the tool that works best for me. There is no single way to do anything. There's nothing more frustrating than trying to do a job with a tool that doesn't fit in your hand. It's all about finding what makes sense and works for you personally.

How to Use This Book

This book has five main sections.

Part one is the introduction, what you're reading right now, which covers the intent of the book and its layout, provides high-level definitions of magic and magic systems, and briefly discusses why you should use *The Magic-System Blueprint* in the first place.

Part two is the Blueprint summary, which takes a quick look at all the components of the Blueprint, what they mean, and how they work. Each piece is discussed briefly to help you get oriented with the information necessary to start using the Blueprint right away.

Part three zooms in for a closer look at each of the Blueprint components and contains the bulk of the book. Each chapter provides a deeper dive into a specific piece of the Blueprint. In these chapters, we will look at the finer details of each component, how these components can impact your story, ways you can tweak and change them, and how they connect with and influence other portions of the Blueprint.

Most chapters in this section will also look at several magic systems and what their Blueprints look like. The same four magic systems are used throughout the book: v from the *Mistborn* series, the magic from *The Lord of the Rings*, the powers of the Marvel Cinematic Universe (MCU), and the technology found in *Stargate SG-1*. I will also reference the Viral Magic System, a magic system I built, to further illustrate how to use and change the pieces of a magic system.

Part four takes a quick look at other things you will need to explore and refine to complete your magic system. *The Magic-System Blueprint* is a powerful tool. Mapping out even a single Blueprint can help you build the vast majority of your magic system, not to mention jump-start your worldbuilding. This is, however, simply a first step. The Blueprint is here to help you understand how the magic functions as a whole. That means some work needs to be done outside the Blueprint to finish your magic system.

Part five of this book contains the appendices. Appendix A is where you will find the Comprehensive Blueprint that you can copy and print off as needed. I even include a link to a PDF version of the document, if that is your preference. Appendix B contains the completed Blueprint for the Viral Magic System I created in 2018.

Again, feel free to jump around to any section that interests you most, but I wouldn't recommend that if this is your first exposure to the Blueprint.

You will learn more, and learn faster, if you print off a copy of the Blueprint and then read this book from start to finish. Once you are familiar with how it all works, this book should function as a reference guide for helping you refresh and utilize the Blueprint for your own systems.

What Is a Magic System?

The term magic system gets tossed around a lot these days, but it's hard to find a clear explanation of what it means. Understanding the definitions of both *magic* and *magic system* is the first step toward building one with intent, clarity, and skill.

Let's start with the basics and build from there.

What Is Magic?

There are dozens of ways to answer this question, but here is the definition I use for magic in works of fiction:

Magic is anything enabling actions beyond our current capability or understanding.

If this seems a tad vague and all-encompassing, that's because it's supposed to be. Many argue that magic must possess some element of mystery or the unexplained, but I disagree. I believe that magic includes everything from hurling fireballs and lightning bolts to force shields and faster-than-light travel. With this definition, the technology and the magic in a work of fiction are treated the same.

This isn't a new concept. Throughout his prolific writing career, science-fiction author Arthur C. Clarke developed principles about science that have become known as Clarke's three laws. The third law is the most widely referenced and the one we are interested in here.

Clarke's Third Law: "Any sufficiently advanced technology is indistinguishable from magic."

The point is, from the right perspective, even the most thought-out, accurate, and realistic technology can be seen as magic. This holds equally true for all kinds of tech, fictional or otherwise.

Fascinatingly enough, this principle can easily be applied in reverse. In fact, there's a line from an online comic called *Girl Genius* that I like to call Agatha's Law, named after the protagonist Agatha Heterodyne.

> **Agatha's Law**: "Any sufficiently analyzed magic is indistinguishable from science."

Magic is the small lie, the alteration, or the piece of imagination accepted, at least in part, by the creator of the magic system and its consumers. Magic, like the very heart of fiction itself, relies on our ability to suspend disbelief and enjoy the result. At their core, alien technology and wizardly magic are, effectively, the same. All that changes is the system around them.

What Is a Magic System?

If magic is anything enabling actions beyond our current capability or understanding, then a magic system can be defined as follows: a magic system is the set of facts and principles that frame the magic and make it understandable to the audience and user.

In other words, any single effect or ability can be magical, and everything managing and explaining it is the system. Using that definition, it is all but impossible to have magic without also having a magic system. Even just displaying an act of magic tells the viewer something about how it works and what it does. It may be a simple or undefined magic system, but it is still a magic system.

With these two definitions in mind, it should be clear that magic and magic systems can be almost anything.

Terrifying monsters that bleed acid? Magic.

Faster-than-light drives that teleport a ship through another dimension? Magic.

Nightmarish men that hunt and kill you in your sleep? Magic.

As you can see, magic can and does appear routinely in science fiction, horror, romance stories, and character dramas. A magic system can be anything you want wherever you need it to be. Don't limit yourself or your readers to just the realms of fantasy.

Of course, I love fantasy stories, so you won't get any complaints from me.

But Why Use the Blueprint?

When it comes down to it, building a magic system and deftly weaving it into a story is hard. It's a process that's easy to start but difficult to master.

It's kind of like constructing a building. Almost anyone can jab a couple of sticks in the ground, throw some cloth over the top, and call it a shelter. Making a building that will fully serve its purpose for decades is something else altogether. The foundation needs to be solid, and the walls need to properly support the weight placed on them, not to mention the planning that goes into plumbing and wiring.

In short, we need to be intentional with our design.

When we build with intent, we can tweak the system to enhance the rest of the story and deliver the precise experience we're looking for.

This doesn't mean having a plan right from the beginning. Some people (weirdos like me) can approach it that way. Others need time to brainstorm, mess around with a few simple concepts and structures. Maybe they even write a full draft of the story first. But at some point, the pieces need to be organized, molded, and placed with deliberation.

This all seems well and good, but what if we want to build something far more wondrous, undefined, or mysterious like in *Harry Potter* or *The Lord of the Rings*? Will *The Magic-System Blueprint* really help with something like that?

Yes. In fact, those kinds of systems take more skill to implement and master than rigorously explained ones.

To build a structure with missing walls, disguised pillars, and secret floors, we need to know exactly what we're doing. If we don't, the odds are good that we'll end up with a pile of rubble instead of the structure we were hoping for.

The Magic-System Blueprint is a tool to help you craft the foundation of information you need to start building with intent. Initially, the Blueprint will provide support as you make your first several attempts at magic-building. Once you grasp the basics, it is still of tremendous use to you. And as your skill increases, the Blueprint will help accelerate the magic-building process and keep you from forgetting important pieces.

I use *The Magic-System Blueprint* because it is the most powerful and flexible tool I have for building magic systems. And it can be for you as well.

PART TWO

Blueprint Summary

The Summary

The Blueprint is a potent tool for designing all the most important aspects of your magic system. It is your guide to mapping out any magic system you want to create, and it can be used to analyze any magic system in existence.

Whether you're building a magic system for a fantasy role-playing game, a thrilling monster movie, or something crazy cool to pump up your sci-fi trilogy, the Blueprint has you covered.

The Blueprint

There's a lot going on here, which is why this portion of the book focuses on introducing all the parts and pieces. We'll look at the components one at a time and get a feel for what they mean and how they might apply to your system.

Note: Even while using the Blueprint, there are bound to be exceptions in the magic system. That is natural and a topic I hope to discuss in greater detail in future works. For now, try not to fixate on those exceptions and focus on what will be true most of the time.

1. Name

This one is about as straightforward as they come. Just put down anything that will help you remember the system and reference it later.

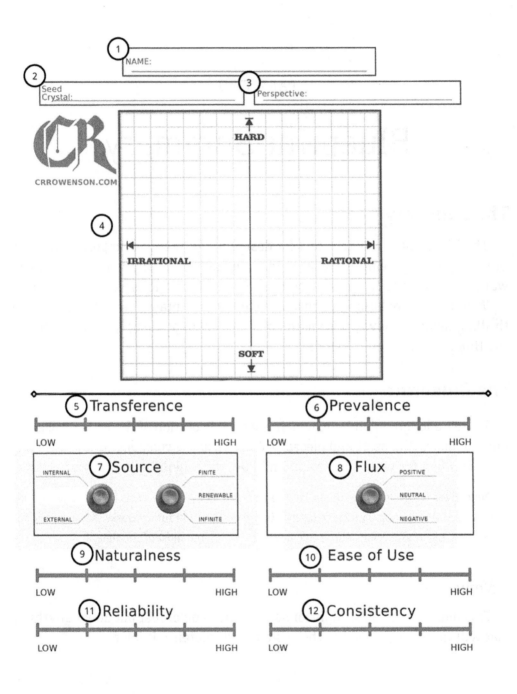

1. NAME:
2. Seed Crystal:
3. Perspective:
4. HARD / IRRATIONAL — RATIONAL / SOFT
5. Transference — LOW / HIGH
6. Prevalence — LOW / HIGH
7. Source — INTERNAL / EXTERNAL — FINITE / RENEWABLE / INFINITE
8. Flux — POSITIVE / NEUTRAL / NEGATIVE
9. Naturalness — LOW / HIGH
10. Ease of Use — LOW / HIGH
11. Reliability — LOW / HIGH
12. Consistency — LOW / HIGH

2. Seed Crystal

The seed crystal is the core concept or point of inspiration around which will grow your entire magic system. This can be almost anything: an image, character idea, or a cool effect. Whatever it is, you want it to be short, powerful, and to the point.

3. Perspective

Perspective is the angle or point of view you are examining the magic system from. Different perspectives will have drastically different views of the magic system and how it works. It is important to establish this before doing any more work on the Blueprint.

4. Types of Magic

Every magic system can be placed in one of four categories determined by a combination of two important attributes.

The hard/soft attribute indicates how much of the system is known or understood, and the rational/irrational attribute indicates how much reason or logic can be applied to its functions.

5. Transference

Transference is all about how the magic effects and abilities are gained, lost, loaned, or stolen from a magic-user. The more readily the power can be picked up, taken away, or shifted around, the greater the level of transference in the system.

6. Prevalence

Prevalence examines how widespread and commonplace the magic is from the chosen perspective. The more common or ubiquitous the magic is within the setting, the greater the prevalence of magic. Systems with little to no presence in the world have a low degree of prevalence.

7. Source

The source variable examines the power within a magic system and identifies where it comes from, how much is present, and whether it can run out or be renewed. It's all about the flow of power from its original form to the production of a magical effect.

8. Flux

Flux is the flow rate of energy into or out of a given system. In this case, we're talking magical energy flowing into or out of the scope of the chosen perspective. If a hero grows in strength throughout a story, then more magic is entering than leaving and the flux is positive. Should more energy be leaving than entering, the hero will decrease in magical power and the flux is negative. In the case that no energy leaves or enters, or the amount leaving equals the amount entering, the flux is neutral.

9. Naturalness

The naturalness variable determines how "natural" or "normal" the magic is compared to the setting around it. Systems with high naturalness feel like a smooth extension of the setting, often blending with other wondrous or strange elements until they are hard to separate from one another. Systems with low naturalness will feel like a bizarre or aberrational addition to the setting.

10. Ease of Use

This variable covers how easy and intuitive it is to effectively utilize the magic in a safe manner. This is yet another sliding scale ranging from easy to difficult. Some magic requires years of training, rare materials, and great personal risk to use effectively. Others can be wielded with a flick of the wrist, the utterance of a single syllable, or even a simple thought.

11. Reliability

Reliability is the extent to which the magic repeatedly reproduces the expected results. As with many of the other variables, this is a sliding scale from high reliability to low reliability. In a high-reliability system, a magic-user can trust the magic to perform the way they need it to when they need it to. If a system has low reliability, the magic-user is gambling that the magic will produce the result they want.

12. Consistency

This variable appears last on the Blueprint for a reason. Consistency looks at all the other variables and pieces of the Blueprint and indicates if they can deviate from their designated placement and by how much. It also takes into account the thematic and tonal consistency across all effects and users within the magic system. If there are a lot of exceptions and outliers in the system, this is how to account for them.

Using the Blueprint

Now that you are familiar with all the bits and bobs of the Blueprint, it's time to make sure you know how to use it.

The Blueprint actually comes in three different forms. The Core Blueprint is the first page, covering everything from the seed crystals to the consistency of the magic. It may seem simple, but this is the true power behind the Blueprint. The Core Blueprint quickly outlines the major shape and tone of the system as a whole. With just a little effort, you can use it to rapidly plan or analyze any system imaginable. Once filled out, the Blueprint will instantly display the difference between two systems that seem otherwise identical.

If the Core Blueprint isn't enough, then you can always step up to the second form: the Essential Blueprint. In addition to all the pieces of the Core Blueprint, the Essential Blueprint has extra pages for recording thoughts and details. There's a lot that goes into each piece of the Blueprint, and it's wonderful to have a place to express why your variables are the way they are.

That brings us to the final format: the Deluxe Blueprint. This version of the Blueprint gives you extra space to record your magical effects and system limitations and examine the balances or imbalances of your system.

Think of the Deluxe Blueprint as the first draft of your magic-system bible. Once you have the Deluxe Blueprint filled out, you can add sections outlining exactly where the magic appears, which characters have what abilities, how you want the magic to tie in to the plot, and so on. Never underestimate the value of having all the information about your magic system in one place.

In the next part of the book, we will dig deeper into each of the previously discussed pieces of the Blueprint. These chapters explore the specifics of each element, what they are, why they're important, and the various ways you can tweak them to your satisfaction. Each chapter will also examine four popular magic systems as examples and provide questions and ideas to help you figure out what to do with your own system.

If this is your first time working with the Blueprint, I suggest you print off a copy and read the book a chapter at a time without skipping around. As you work your way through, try filling out the Blueprint for your own magic system. This book was designed to function as a reference guide. Once you know the ins and outs of the Blueprint and what it can do, you can jump to any chapter if you need clarification or a refresher.

Now let's get into the details!

PART THREE

The Details

B Y THIS POINT, you should have a basic understanding of what the Blueprint is, how it can help you, and what the various parts and pieces mean. In this next part of the book, we are digging deep into the components of the Blueprint to explore them in detail.

Each component has its own chapter, and most chapters follow the same structure with the following sections.

What Is It?

This section briefly explains the piece being discussed. It is approximately the same length as the definition found in the Blueprint Summary and is here to provide all the information in one place to make future referencing easier.

The Details

Here we examine you guessed it the specifics of the piece in question, diving further into what it is and how to approach it.

Impact on Your Story

Magic systems are powerful, transformative tools in our fiction. Here we will look at the primary ways the magic system component influences the story and the world around it.

Examples

Throughout the book, we will return to the same four systems to solidify our understanding of the Blueprint. The systems covered will be Allomancy from the *Mistborn* series by Brandon Sanderson, *The Lord of the Rings* by J. R. R. Tolkien, Phase One of the Marvel Cinematic Universe (up through the first *Avengers* movie), and *Stargate SG-1*.

How to Change It

With a firm understanding of topic at hand, it's time to discuss how we can twist and reshape the magic system into what we need it to be. There will be references to my own Viral Magic System and additional examples to illustrate the point and spark ideas.

Blueprint Connections

Every part of the Blueprint is tied together, but some pieces have stronger connections than others. Here we will identify which of the other components has a strong influence on, or is strongly influenced by, the component at hand.

It's time to get into the details. If you haven't already, now would be the time to print out a copy of the Blueprint from the back of the book and fill it out as you read.

Names

What Is It?

This is where you develop your reference name for the magic system itself. This could be the name of the magic system, the scientific term for the monster you're creating, or even the manufacturer responsible for making all the advanced gadgets in your universe. Some people use descriptive or attributional naming. In this case, the name isn't a fabricated word but rather something that captures the heart of what the magic is, does, and represents.

As long as you know what it means, it will work just fine.

Details

The important thing with the name is to not overthink it. I know, pretty rich coming from me, but it's true.

What's that Shakespeare quote? "The blood of an enemy, no matter their name, will taste just as sweet." Something like that?

The point is, while names can have power, they are also arbitrary and pointless on their own. They provide value to a magic system by allowing the audience and characters in the story to reference the system quickly and succinctly.

There are a couple of general approaches people take when naming their magic system. I use attributional naming a lot, especially when in the early stages of development. My systems tend to have names like Viral Magic, Organ Magic, and Nano-Magic. Completely useless on their own, but they still allow me to keep the differing systems straight and quickly communicate my concepts and vision with others.

There's no limit to the methods for generating names. We can combine differ-ent root words and suffixes together (Allomancy equals *alloy* plus *-mancy*). We can describe the magic system as actions (rune stitching), or create entirely new words (Patronus), or even just name the individual pieces instead of the system as a whole (Iron Man, Thor).

But here's the dirty secret: it doesn't matter what you pick!

Yes, a good name can evoke thoughts, images, and emotions. And, yes, a good name can represent an entire character, series, or genre. That said, there is no right name. Remember what Shakespeare said about blood I'm pretty sure that quote is about blood. The name is just a reference. The power is in the magic system itself.

We should still do our best to come up with interesting names for our magic systems, but it's not worth stressing or losing sleep over. Names and ideas come with time. Start with something simple so you can keep track of what you're talking about and keep moving forward. And you can always change it if you find something better in the future.

Seed Crystal

What Is It?

The terminology may seem a little bizarre, but check this out: Crystals can't form without a substrate or particle to grow from. Laboratories use tiny crystals as the starting point to quickly grow larger, uniform crystals. These tiny starters are called seed crystals, and they provide the structure necessary for rapid growth.

We need the same thing for your magic system: a single point of inspiration around which the structure can grow. This can be an image, a plot hook, a setting element, a specific magical effect, or even a powerful character moment.

The Details

Having a good seed crystal is far more valuable than it might seem at first. Yes, magic systems can grow and form naturally with enough time and brainstorming, but the seed crystal can act as a powerful force multiplier.

While it doesn't have a direct impact on your story, a seed crystal can act as your North Star and guiding light during the development of your magic system. If you know your seed crystal, then you know what excites you from the beginning and can tap into that excitement for inspiration any time the creation process drags you down. Not only will this give you a consistent font of inspiration, but by holding the seed firmly in your mind while building, ideas will come more readily, decisions will be easier to make, and the entire process will go faster.

Cool, right?

A seed crystal can be almost anything and come from literally anywhere. The important thing is that it generates ideas. Character concepts, visuals, video games, other novels, TV shows, movies, comic books, strong emotions, tense situations, global conflicts, and defining moments can all serve as seed crystals. Don't hesitate to reach outside the realm of fiction either. As a human being, you have a vast well of experience and knowledge to draw from. Look to subjects you are familiar with and skills you are well versed in. These can easily form the foundation of a good seed crystal.

When first starting a new magic system or story, it's fairly common to have several sources of inspiration. There's nothing wrong with that, but if we try to follow too many guiding lights at once, we might end up just as lost as if we didn't have any at all. Whenever possible, it's better to combine and consolidate the multiple sources of inspiration down into a single, simple point.

That's why there's just a single line for your seed crystal on the Blueprint. It might be a challenge, but getting the entire seed to fit in this limited space means it has to be all the more powerful.

Examples

Unfortunately, no matter how much I wish it to be otherwise, I did not write the *Mistborn* series. Nor did I direct the *Lord of the Rings* movies, manage the Marvel Cinematic Universe, or write for *Stargate SG-1*. I wasn't even a consultant on any of these amazing projects. While I cannot tell you what the seed crystals for these magic systems were, I can still give you some examples.

While working on my Viral Magic System, my seed crystal was the idea of special viruses that make people sick but also grant them special powers. This helped me cut out ideas and effects that were interesting but didn't contribute to the core concept.

Other seed crystals might be a living desert invading the surrounding land; a warehouse filled with dangerous, historical artifacts; a character exiled and hunted for pursuing reviled arts; magic based on paint-making; an international war over a magical resource; trees with magical defense mechanisms; or a magic-user encased in ice slamming into an armored tank.

Each of these could easily serve as the seed crystal for multiple magic systems, and they can be tweaked and altered to create something truly unique.

Blueprint Connections

Obviously, the seed crystal we choose will have a massive impact on the system as a whole. Pick something creepy and gross, which is one hundred percent my brand, and you'll likely end up with a creepy and gross magic system. Exactly how it connects to the rest of the Blueprint depends entirely on the seed itself. Some seed crystals will naturally address certain parts of the Blueprint or steer the settings in a particular direction.

For example, let's say our seed crystal is quantum computers. Without deciding anything else, the system is likely to end up with higher transference and reliability. A computer is not built solely for its original creator. How widespread could computing become if it only ever functioned for the one person that created it? And what good would a computer be if its performance and behavior weren't reliable?

What if, instead of quantum computers, we picked the seed crystal of organ harvesting from magical creatures? That system is likely to have a higher naturalness because it all comes from creatures living in the wild. If the beasts are being hunted to extinction, the system will have negative flux as well.

Find a simple yet evocative seed crystal, and everything else that follows will be easier.

Perspective

What Is It?

Perspective tells us what point of view we are adopting while examining a magic system and frames the extent of our vision while we map out the Blueprint.

As the creators, how we see and experience the magic system is different from how our readers will see and experience it. Because we built the system, we know more about it than anyone else. That changes our understanding of how the system works, looks, and feels. What seems like a well-documented and highly scientific magic system to us might come across as a mysterious and unknowable force to our readers.

When we say that magic is anything enabling actions beyond our current capability or understanding, perspective tells us exactly whose capability or understanding we're talking about. Perspective is, in my opinion, one of the most important and useful pieces of the Blueprint for exploring and building a magic system.

The Details

Before digging into the rest of the Blueprint, we need to establish the angle we are observing and analyzing from. By defining the perspective, we can jump into the point of view of our target audience, a single character, or even an entire nation within the story world. We can even use perspective to control how much of the system we examine at one time, allowing us to consider the system in its entirety or focus in on specific portions of the system.

I'd avoid using the perspective of this C. R. Rowenson guy I know, though. He's just plain weird.

It's important to note that scope is also a part of the perspective. In addition to observing the magic system through anyone's eyes, we can focus on as much or as little of the system as we like. In some cases, we need to zoom in on a very specific effect or ability. Other times might call for examining a particular branch or subsystem of the magic.

When using the Blueprint to map a new system, I recommend adopting the creator perspective and looking at the system in its entirety. This will be the most natural perspective for you to adopt and will provide the greatest benefit the fastest. As the creator, you will know the most about the magic system, including all the bits and pieces that won't make it into the story. If you have multiple magic systems in your world, just focus on one of them for now.

If the creator perspective feels incomplete, consider mapping out multiple Blueprints from additional perspectives. In part four of the book, we'll take a quick look at the universal perspective, the audience perspective, the protagonist perspective, and the antagonist perspective, but those are just a few of the options. You can always map out a Blueprint for each major demographic in your story so you understand how they view and experience your system. This can be incredibly useful, but it is something you should do only after mapping a Blueprint from the creator perspective.

Examples

Let's take a quick look at each of the example systems and the perspectives I adopt while analyzing them.

Mistborn by Brandon Sanderson (Audience Perspective)

While analyzing the magic of *Mistborn*, my perspective is that of a reader. I cannot adopt the creator perspective as I am not Brandon Sanderson and I did not write these books (and time-travel has done nothing to change this). I could take the perspective of one of the characters in the story, but for simplicity I'll stick with my natural perspective as a member of the audience.

As for the scope, there are three different magic systems in the *Mistborn* series. For the sake of simplicity, we are going to focus on Allomancy. We will also limit ourselves to the information covered in the first three *Mistborn* novels.

The Lord of the Rings (Audience Perspective)

While mapping out the magic in *The Lord of the Rings*, my perspective was that of a member of the audience who had watched the extended edition of all three movies. This perspective does not consider any lore from any of the video games, *The Silmarillion*, the books themselves, or any other works or notes by Tolkien. The perspective could easily be changed to include these additional sources, but again, for simplicity, this analysis will be limited to the movies.

Lastly, my Blueprint of the magic system from *The Lord of the Rings* considers all natural powers of various beings and the One Ring. There are many cases where the Rings of Power run counter to the rest of the world, and I have done my best to consider everything as a singular whole instead of individual elements.

Marvel Cinematic Universe (Audience Perspective)

This one is especially straightforward. My perspective while mapping this system was that of a viewer who has seen only the movies. It does not take into account any knowledge from comic books or related media. It also takes into account only the movies up to and including the first *Avengers* movie.

Depending on how you look at it, each hero could be considered as a separate system. For our purposes, I examine the universe as a whole, considering everything we see all at once and tying it together.

Stargate SG-1 (Audience Perspective)

My perspective when analyzing the technology in *Stargate SG-1* is that of a viewer of the show. I do not delve into anything brought up in Stargate Atlantis, on the fan pages, or any supplemental material. My analysis is also limited to the technology alone. It does not include or cover the abilities of the Ascended, the Ori, or specific racial abilities as these can be considered distinct magic systems.

Blueprint Connections

The perspective we set when mapping a Blueprint affects *the entire Blueprint*. The prevalence of the magic, where it comes from, the flux of power, and even the system's position on the hard/soft and rational/irrational axes all are influenced by the perspective. What you may view as a hard-rational system with overall negative flux may come across to the reader as a soft-irrational with a neutral flux. The main character, living with the magic, might see the same system as being soft-rational with a positive flux as they personally grow in power.

Perspective is connected to everything, and that's what makes it so stinking cool!

The exact nature of these connections is something you will have to learn for yourself as you practice and gain experience. The more perspectives you utilize, the better you will comprehend how your magic looks and feels, as well as what it represents to various people. From there you can alter your design to enhance or minimize different pieces of the system to deliver the exact experience you want.

For now, the creator perspective will provide the fewest complications for you and your magic system.

Types of Magic Intro

EVERY MAGIC system can be placed in one of four categories determined by a combination of two important attributes: how well known or understood the magic is (hard/soft) and how logical it is or how much reason can be applied to its functions (rational/irrational).

When combined, these two attributes illuminate the type of magic a system belongs to. I have found it easiest to visualize them using the chart found near the top of the Blueprint.

With that in place, it's easy to see that the four types of magic systems are hard-rational, hard-irrational, soft-rational, and soft-irrational. This probably doesn't make much sense on its own, which is why we're going to spend the next two chapters digging into each axis and discussing what they mean for the system as a whole. Once we understand these pieces, we can look at the four types of magic systems and how they can impact and improve our stories.

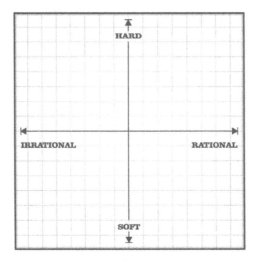

Hard and Soft Magic

What Is It?

The hard/soft axis is a sliding scale that indicates how much of the magic system is known or understood. The more someone knows or understands, the harder a system becomes from their perspective.

Imagine your magic system is a tangible, three-dimensional Thing. Now imagine pulling out a camera and taking a picture of that Thing. Then, some-how, all other memories of the Thing are erased. Everything we know about the Thing exists in that one photograph. The more of the Thing that is visible, in focus, and identifiable within the picture, the harder and more defined the Thing seems. If only some of the Thing is captured in frame, obscured by other objects, or even if the image is just fuzzy or out of focus, it seems softer and more abstract.

The photo is our perspective, and the Thing is the actual magic system.

The Details

How hard or soft a magic system is depends on how much is known or understood, but what does that mean exactly? What is there to know?

Well . . . everything. What different effects exist in the system? What are the boundaries and limitations of the magic system? How much do other people know about it? Does someone from the chosen perspective know the magic exists? What are the underlying patterns and themes of the magic? Are there underlying patterns and themes to the magic? How does someone go about using the magic? Can someone counter or interrupt the magic? Are you sick of these open-ended rhetorical questions yet?

What we're talking about is the entire Blueprint itself and the magic system it represents. Larger and more complex systems will have more information to absorb and process than smaller, simpler systems. Given everything there is to know about a system, how much of it does someone from the specified perspective actually know and understand?

There are two ways we can go about this analysis. One is to think in terms of percentages. Returning to the earlier photo analogy, what percentage of the total system is captured within the frame of the photo? Thirty percent? Fifty-five percent? Ninety-eight percent? This percentage correlates directly to the sliding scale of hard and soft magic. Larger percentages are harder and lower percentages are softer.

This is fairly easy to manage when we're talking high or low numbers. If only 10 percent is known, then it's clearly a soft magic system. If 80 percent is known, then it's a hard magic system.

Some magic systems fall closer to the middle of the spectrum, and that's where things get a bit muddy. Do we know 55 percent of the system or only 45 percent? In these cases, it's useful to examine this aspect of the magic system as a binary relationship. Forget the scale and ask whether it's harder than it is soft? Do we know the majority of the system or the minority? That should give you the answer you need to place your system and keep moving forward with the rest of the Blueprint.

When mapping a system from the creator perspective, which I highly recommend for your first time, there are additional things to consider.

First, how complex do we want the system to be? Is this a massive god-machine of a system with a million moving pieces all pushing, pulling, and turning one another at once? Or is it just a red button and a blue button, each producing a specific magical effect? It's easy to make the button system feel hard. Explain one button and what it does and you're already 50 percent there. The god-machine? That's likely to stay a soft system no matter how much we learn and share.

Second, how much of the system do we, as a creator, actually need to know? If there are just two buttons, we should probably know what both of them do. With the god-machine, we can get away with focusing on the general trends and specific pieces that will be important to the story. Not every magic system needs to be a hard magic system; we don't need to know everything.

Finally, what we see and know is not what the reader sees and knows. More than that, what they know and understand will change as they read a story or view a series. The more they learn, the harder the magic will become to them. That said, because they rely on the creator to explain the system, the system can never be harder for them than it is for us, the creator.

Impact on Your Story

This is a lot to consider, and it can be difficult to wrap our heads around. So why bother at all?

How hard or soft a system is has a massive impact on how the magic can be used to progress the plot and solve plot problems. Harder systems can solve bigger plot problems. If we solve a large plot problem without a sufficiently hard magic system, our readers will feel confused, upset, and even robbed of an important moment.

I love the *Lord of the Rings* movies, but this conversation wouldn't be complete without discussing the giant eagles.

Yes, we're going to talk a little trash about Granddad Tolkien. Please don't lynch me!

In the story, Gandalf escapes Saruman's tower by leaping over the edge onto the back of a giant eagle. Then, at the very end, he swoops in on another eagle to pull Frodo and Sam from the slopes of Mount Doom.

Why didn't they use the eagles to begin with?! Why spend 686 minutes remember, we're watching the extended editions on this epic journey if they could have simply summoned flying mounts to take them there? It seems ridiculous!

But it just seems that way because of how little we know of the magic in the world. There is actually a plethora of world-building and magic reasons why riding the eagles to Mordor wasn't an option, but because the magic system is so soft, we don't know any of them, which can lead to some major frustration.

Let's look at another example: A powerful necromancer has risen in the west, their army of dead grows every day, and the heroes need to travel across the land and put a stop to this evil power once and for all. The main characters then spend three books navigating past dangers untold and hardships unnumbered, defeating undead minions the entire way to finally arrive in the necromancer's throne room . . . and then one of the characters uses a power we've never seen or heard of, and defeats the necromancer with a wave of their hand.

I don't know about you, but that book would be sailing across the room and into a trash can before the first round of huzzahs from the heroes.

To avoid this, it's best to think of it as foreshadowing. If the character is facing a problem for the entire book and you want magic to be the solution, you better foreshadow the solution well in advance. That is most easily achieved by making a harder system. On the other hand, if a problem is going to come and go in a few paragraphs, you can freely use magic to solve it without much foreshadowing.

As you might imagine, building a sufficiently hard magic system is the key to satisfying problem-solving. Harder magic systems also work better for setting up good plot twists and puzzles. The key is making sure your magic never robs the characters or readers of an important or powerful moment.

Examples

Mistborn (Hard Magic)

Allomancy from the *Mistborn* series is an outstanding example of a hard magic system.

In the beginning of the first book of the series, the magic is vague and unclear, but powerful. This changes when we, the readers, learn that one of the main characters, Vin, is a Mistborn, a special kind of magic-user with access to all the powers. At this point, the story dives into a delightful training sequence that outlines the majority of the magic system.

Within a single chapter, the reader is exposed to the eight base metals and the magical effects they produce. At this point, the reader knows most of what there is to know about Allomancy. There are only a few pieces left to learn, and all the rules make the learning curve short, which is perfect for a hard magic system.

But Sanderson doesn't reveal all the system yet. In fact, there are a few pieces that don't get revealed, displayed, or even mentioned until later in the series. Even with those hidden elements, we know roughly 80 percent of the system by the end of the first book.

Of course, that is purely from my perspective as a reader. If we change the lens through which we observe the magic, the system appears quite different. The nobles of the world are all aware of the magic, but there are many misconceptions and misunderstandings about the details of the system. To your average member of a Great House, the magic is still hard, but it's not as hard as it is for us as the readers.

Change the perspective to that of Skaa, a nonmagical member of the slave caste, and everything is radically different. Most of the population has no clue that the power exists, let alone what it can do or how it works. They simply know that some people have strange and dangerous powers. For them, this could be an incredibly soft magic system while being a hard system for the protagonist.

The Lord of the Rings (Soft Magic)

Even to this day, the magic found in Tolkien's work is the exemplar for soft and mysterious magic systems. In fact, the magic system in this series is about as soft as it can possibly be without taking all instances of magic "off-screen" altogether.

Between the One Ring, Gandalf, Galadriel, Saruman, the Ringwraiths, and other magical creatures, magic pops up now and then throughout the entire trilogy. But those displays of magic are few and far between, and we seldom see the same effect twice. Overall, we as the audience are given no hints as to the scope of the magic, precious few examples of magical effects, and even fewer explanations.

A sense of mystery and wonder to the world of Middle-earth is what solidifies the magic in *The Lord of the Rings* as a soft system, at least for us as members of the audience.

But what if we change our perspective to others within Middle-earth? What happens then?

Well, it will depend on where they live, but normal people living their lives are aware of magic and the strangeness of their world. While the average denizen might know more of the scope of the magic through rumors, stories, and legend, it's unlikely that they know the details any better than we do.

But if we pick up the perspective of Gandalf, Galadriel, or Saruman, things are bound to change. As magic-users, they are going to have a deeper understanding of what they can and cannot do than the audience could possibly have. They know more things about the world, the shifts of power, and how the power can be used than we do. There's no way to be sure how far this would shift the magic up the spectrum, but it is certainly a much harder magic system to Gandalf than it is to us. After all, Gandalf knows when and where he can get help from the giant eagles. We don't.

The perspective we use in this book is as members of an audience who have watched only the three movies (the extended editions, we're not heathens). If we went out and picked up a copy of *The Silmarillion*, that would change things. There is information in that book about the creation of the world and the nature of magic that you can't, as far as I'm aware, find anywhere else. Adding this information to our perspective would make the magic system seem harder and more defined.

Marvel Cinematic Universe (Hard Magic)

Let's take stock. By the end of Phase One, we have a variety of heroes in the ranks: Thor, the demigod; Iron Man, the genius inventor in a superpowered flight suit; Captain America, the super soldier; Hulk, a giant rage monster; Hawkeye, a master bowman; and Black Widow, assassin extraordinaire.

Throughout the previous solo Marvel movies, each hero was introduced, their powers explained, and their limits explored. By the time *The Avengers* rolls around, we know what they can and cannot do, and there are no surprises. At least not from our heroes.

While Loki, the main villain of *The Avengers*, doesn't show us much about himself that we haven't already seen, he does bring new magical artifacts and effects onto the scene. One is a scepter that can twist the hearts of man to become devoted to Loki and his plan. He also steals an artifact introduced in earlier movies and uses it to open a portal between worlds and create force fields.

As members of the audience, we start *The Avengers* already knowing the majority of the system. There are some new features, true, but by the end of the movie we know a great deal more about those as well. This all makes for a hard magic system, but it's not quite that simple.

While we know the majority of the magic we see and experience in *The Avengers*, what about everything else in the MCU? New heroes, villains, aliens, and powerful forces are being uncovered and revealed with each installment in the series. More importantly, thanks to the end-credit scenes, we know that more will be revealed in the future. In that sense, what we are seeing is likely a small piece of a much larger whole.

And wouldn't that make it a soft magic system? Yes, potentially, but the writers of the Marvel Cinematic Universe put a great deal of effort into making sure we know as much about the magic system as we can at a given time, without completely spoiling the plot, of course. Additionally, because of how the magic is managed and introduced, these formerly unknown pieces feel more like system growth, which is a separate piece of the Blueprint, than something that has been there all along.

If the massive scope of the universe were clear from day one, this would likely be a soft system. But that is not the case. New elements of magic are introduced and explored in small bites, allowing the MCU to remain a hard magic system in the eyes of the audience. Altogether, this points to a magic system that bounces between 50 and 75 percent along the hard/soft spectrum.

Even if we shift perspectives, this assessment of the magic system doesn't change much. Each of the heroes understands more about their own powers and the powers of their allies than we do, but they also know less about the villains and their allies than we do. Even if we switch our perspective to that of an average human in the MCU version of Earth, the magic remains fairly hard. Sure, they don't know the heroes' powers as well as we do, but they are certainly aware of them. And I'd be shocked there weren't hundreds of websites documenting, tracking, and theorizing the capabilities of these heroes.

In both cases, the placement does shift. The hero's perspective is a harder magic system, and a citizen's perspective is a softer magic system. In all cases, the magic is managed and introduced in such a way that it remains in the medium-high range of the hard/soft scale.

Stargate SG-1 (Soft Magic)

Given that *Stargate SG-1* clearly falls in the science fiction camp, one might expect the technology to be a hard system, but it is actually soft. Much of this comes down to the presentation and how large the system feels.

From the very start of the show even before that, if we count the movie we learn that the universe is a massive place filled with more technology and species than we thought possible. The main characters and the audience are often introduced to incredible forms of technology as the show goes on.

While each piece we see increases our knowledge and hardens the system, our understanding of the complete system remains meager. There is no telling what else might exist out in the universe. No matter how much we learn about the Stargates, ship drives, and other tools and tech, the show makes it clear that humanity is only scratching the surface of what the magic can do.

That may seem a little confusing, especially compared to the MCU. Both are expansive fictional universes filled with magic. How can one be hard and the other soft? Well, part of it is the scope. Because of how it was written, *Stargate SG-1* feels much stranger and unexplored than the MCU. It is also because while the MCU starts small and continues to grow, everything in the Stargate universe existed from the beginning and is waiting to be discovered.

All of this combines into a wonderfully soft and mysterious magic system that is *Stargate SG-1*. At the very least, it is softer than it is hard.

Unlike the MCU, a change in perspective here could mean a radical shift on this scale. Normal citizens of Earth know almost nothing about what exists around them. They have the same technology and knowledge we have in our own world, and that's it. That's about as soft as it gets.

If we jump to the perspective of an alien race such as the Goa'uld, the Asgardians, or the Ancients, things shift in the opposite direction. In the Stargate universe, humans from earth are still new to the galactic arena and sit far behind the other races both in terms of knowledge and capability. These other races know their technology the way we know automobiles and polymer science. It is a much harder magic system to them than it is to us in the audience.

How to Change It

There are a number of ways we can move and shift our magic system up and down the hard/soft spectrum. The most obvious solution, and the solution most authors turn to, is to simply explain more or less of the magic system. Showing and explaining less shifts it toward the soft end of the spectrum, and showing or explaining more shifts it toward the hard end of the spectrum.

This can work, but it needs to be done with the utmost care. When we explain less, we run the risk of frustrating and confusing our readers. That should happen only when we want it to. Writers are jerks like that. It's part of the job description.

What's more, previously awesome and powerful story moments and plot twists suddenly cease to make any kind of sense. Sometimes a lack of detail will even create plot holes. Imagine if earlier drafts of *The Lord of the Rings* had included explanations about the giant eagles, but then Tolkien decided to cut that nugget of information, hoping to make the eagles' arrival seem wondrous and incredible. Just like that, a new plot hole is born.

We need to be careful when attempting the opposite as well. Explanations can increase the risk of generating the dreaded information dump. The information shouldn't be there for the sake of being there. It must serve a role in the story and not disrupt the audience's immersion. This is a tricky beast to manage, and sometimes we're better off making a system harder in another way.

Fortunately, there are plenty of options.

For one, we can manage the overall complexity of the system. Remember the button magic, where there are just two buttons and two magical effects? By pressing one button, we learn about half the system. That's what we're talking about here. If we simplify our system by cutting down on the number of magical effects, simplifying the rules, and minimizing contradictions, then it takes less explanation to make the system harder.

And the other direction is just as simple. Make the current system a subsystem of a larger whole. Add more rules, patterns, effects, or applications. Larger systems require more information to reach the tipping point between soft and hard magic systems, which means more words and more story.

The best way to control the audience's perception of a hard or soft magic system is through the protagonist. If we make the protagonist a magic-user, the magic is going to become a harder system. In a story with a close narrative style, the reader likely spends all their time in the protagonist's head. As the protagonist uses the magic, learns more about it, and grows in their understanding of it, so does the reader. In reverse, we can make a system feel softer to the reader by making sure the protagonist does not or cannot use magic.

When you're exploring the magic from some perspective other than as the creator, consider changing the awareness from that perspective. This can be done both on a micro and macro level. It's easy enough to build a hidden world or a deep conspiracy. In fact, there are entire genres focused around exactly that kind of setup.

Going the other way isn't difficult either. Pushing the magic into the realm of common knowledge is easy to do and opens up all kinds of options for your stories.

It's also worth considering how long the magic has been around and how easily it can be accessed. The longer people have been exposed to it, the more likely it is that they have studied and learned about it. Old and ubiquitous magic interwoven into everyday life usually feels harder because the characters understand it better. If the magic is new or long forgotten, then nobody is going to know what it is or what it does, making it a softer system.

This doesn't work for the creator perspective, as the age of the magic should not affect our personal understanding of the system, so we need only consider this aspect when exploring different perspectives.

Blueprint Connections

Perspective

The perspective we select when mapping out a magic system does more to influence its placement on the hard/soft spectrum than anything else. Each character, organization, and nation will have different levels of knowledge about the system. The audience's understanding of the magic system will be different from our own. The knowledge possessed by a trained mage will be different from that possessed by a king or baker.

The Rational/Irrational Scale

The rational/irrational scale tells us whether we can apply reason and logic. The hardness and rationality of a magic system are closely linked. They are distinct elements of the magic system, but they can be difficult to separate from each other. As our knowledge of the magic increases, so does its rationality.

With the right knowledge, a ten-digit number shifts from a random sequence to a way to telephone a friend. Add more knowledge into the mix and those previously random numbers can tell us where in the country the phone number routes to and even which central office or exchange code it belongs to. Knowledge can quickly turn random noise into recognizable patterns.

This relationship, however, goes one way. Knowing and understanding often makes a magic system more rational. But making a magic system more rational on its own doesn't mean the creator, the reader, or anyone else knows more about the system itself.

Reliability

The more we understand what the magic can do, what it can't do, and how it works, the more readily we can apply that knowledge to get what we want. Reliability is all about the chances of getting what we want out of the magic. Some factors of reliability are beyond the influence of the hard/soft axis, but others are not.

For example, knowing how a car engine works can lead to greater reliability. We know how to make minor repairs and what the engine can handle, but this doesn't stop the engine from breaking down or behaving oddly sometimes. Knowledge and understanding alone can make something only so reliable.

Prevalence

Repeated exposure and large data samples make it easier to spot hidden patterns and correlations. Exposure to a magic system means the time to study it, so the more prevalent and widespread the magic is, the harder the magic system is likely to be to people in the world.

There is magic in *The Lord of the Rings*, but we in the audience don't see it very often. Because we rarely see it, it's difficult to determine what is actually a pattern and what is a random occurrence. In the *Mistborn* saga, the readers are heavily exposed to the magic, both in application and in theory. It's no wonder why Allomancy feels so much harder than the magic in *The Lord of the Rings*.

Ease of Use

Some systems have a stronger connection between applicability and the hard/soft scale than others. If knowledge and understanding is critical for the use of magic, then the system will need to be harder in order for characters to use it properly. If the magic is used purely through instinct, then the hardness of the magic might not factor in at all. It really comes down to what the magic-user needs in order to wield the system.

This correlation doesn't always carry over to the reader. It is possible for the magic to be hard to the character and soft to the reader. Imagine a story where wizards study for decades to produce even the smallest magical effects. In this case, the magic system might be quite hard to the character. But the reader doesn't need to know all the details. The creator can provide narrative coverage to indicate the character's knowledge without explicitly spelling it out.

Naturalness

Similar to the prevalence of a magic system, high levels of naturalness often lead to harder magic systems. If the magic is a natural, integrated part of the setting, then studying and learning about the world will also teach the audience something about the magic.

Rational/Irrational Magic

What Is It?

The rational/irrational axis is a sliding scale indicating to what degree one can apply logic and reason to a magic system. With a rational system, people can use what they already know to logically predict unseen functions, rules, or applications of the magic.

Let's repeat what we did in the chapter on the hard/soft axis and imagine your magic system as a concrete, tangible Thing we can photograph and analyze. What does it look like? Does it have geometric patterns or a repeating structural element, or is it all non-Euclidian shapes and abstract curves? Can someone use what they see to anticipate how the Thing looks and feels outside the frame of the photo?

That's what the rational/irrational spectrum is all about.

The Details

To reiterate, a magic system is rational if it is built with, and functions in accordance with, reason and logic. Anyone interacting with the magic system the reader, a character, even the creator can extrapolate and predict unseen portions of the system.

On the flip side, an irrational magic system was not built with, and does not function in accordance with, reason or logic. In this case, someone interacting with the magic knows something is true only when they see or in the creator's case, decide that it is true. Even then, they know the truth only as they see it and cannot extrapolate further.

When trying to build a rational magic system, the knee-jerk reaction is often to fill it with rules and limitations. That can help. In fact, rules, limitations, and patterns are important parts of any rational magic system, but they're only parts of it. Rules and limitations alone don't make a system rational. The rules need to be connected and allow for further application of logic.

Let's revisit the two-button magic system. The user has a red button and a blue button, and each generates a single magical effect. When they press the red button, flames erupt from the ground before them.

Even with this minimal amount of information, there are several logical assumptions a user might make. If the red button creates flame effect, then the blue button might create a water or ice effect. One might also assume that the flames they saw behave just like any other flame. The gouts of fire could be used to heat a kettle, cook a steak, or light a cigar. One might even assume that there is a reserve of fuel somewhere feeding the fire as long as the red button is pressed.

These assumptions make perfect sense given what we know of the world around us. If the magic holds to these patterns, then it is a rational magic system that adheres to logic and reason. But if the blue button creates a pillar of stone, the flames produce no heat, or if no fuel is consumed by the fire, then the chains of logic have been broken or ignored. That means the system is irrational.

No magic system is quite that straightforward, but the more logical patterns it follows, the more rational a magic system it is. But every hole you add to logic or reason behind a magic system increases its irrationality.

It is important to note that the adherence to logic and reason applies to more than just the magic system itself. The system, its rules, the related effects, and the limitations may all be perfectly rational, but we also need to consider its application. Once we know the magic can generate a specific effect, can we apply reason to find new and creative uses for that effect?

For example, if we have a magic knife that cuts smoothly through stone, it would be fair to assume it can cut through substances like wood and cloth just as easily. That's a rational assumption to make. If the knife cuts stone and only stone, then we can't extrapolate further and can trust only in what is already established. All we've got is one irrational knife.

I bet that's a sentence you never expected to read in your lifetime.

Impact on Your Story

More than anything, the rational/irrational axis changes how cohesive and connected the magic system seems to us, our readers, and our characters. Rational systems generally feel more understandable, like a single cohesive unit. Irrational systems often feel like a cluster of unique, maybe even random, effects and abilities. Without logic and reason holding them together, irrational systems can also make your setting feel alien and incomprehensible.

With a rational magic system, we can take information we already have and predict how other pieces of the system might work before actually seeing them work. That becomes important if we intend to use the magic in creative ways. Sure, the blue key opens the blue door, but if we change the color of the key, will it open other doors? If the magic-user cannot follow logical assumptions to a correct outcome, they will struggle to solve problems in new ways.

On a similar note, more rational magic systems make our characters seem cerebral and clever. A rational magic system that relies on skill and cleverness will complement and spotlight curious, quick-thinking, and intelligent characters. An irrational system, on the other hand, might draw more attention to characters with power, intense emotions, or strong convictions. It's all in how you present it.

Examples

Mistborn (Rational Magic)

Remember, the placement of a magic system along the rational/irrational scale is determined by the presence of underlying logic or patterns in the system. If it is rational, a magic-user or reader should be able to extrapolate information about the magic system. It just so happens that this perfectly describes Allomancy.

If you've read any book by Brandon Sanderson, it should be no surprise that Allomancy is a highly rational magic system. Clever heroes who use the rules of magic in creative but logical ways are foundational to Sanderson's style.

In the *Mistborn* series, we learn early in the first book that certain magic-users can burn iron to pull on nearby metal and burn steel to push it away. With that information, we can think of a dozen applications deflecting arrows, pulling swords off the ground that actually work. Some of these examples even appear later in the story.

In addition to its highly logical application of effects, Allomancy has an underlying structure holding it all together. The Allomantic metals fall into one of five categories based their effects: physical, enhancement, mental, temporal, or God. With the exception of the God Metals, each of these categories is then split into four quadrants. Each quadrant is a specific subcategory that indicates whether the effect is internal or external and whether the effect is pushing or pulling.

Physical Powers

Internal / Pushing	Internal / Pulling
External / Pushing	External / Pulling

Mental Powers

Internal / Pushing	Internal / Pulling
External / Pushing	External / Pulling

Internal / Pushing	Internal / Pulling
External / Pushing	External / Pulling

Internal / Pushing	Internal / Pulling
External / Pushing	External / Pulling

Enhancement Powers

Temporal Powers

The Lord of the Rings (Irrational Magic)

The magic in *The Lord of the Rings* is a terrific example of an irrational magic system. We can't predict what might be out there beyond what is shown to us. We can't even develop creative applications for the magical effects we do see. We know that Gandalf broke the stone bridge of Khazad-d m, but we can't assume he can break other types of stone in other locations. The magic simply isn't consistent enough to be sure of it.

We know what the magic in *The Lord of the Rings* can do only when we see it happen. From our perspective as the audience, there are no theories to apply, patterns to follow, or repetition to rely on. That's all there is to it, and there's absolutely nothing wrong with that. Irrational magic systems in fiction are just as valuable as rational systems.

Marvel Cinematic Universe (Irrational Magic)

At first glance, the magic from the Marvel Cinematic Universe seems difficult to pin down. Each hero's powers seem thematically consistent with themselves and can be applied in unique and clever ways. As members of the audience, we can daydream previously unseen uses of their powers with some success. But there's more to it than that.

In the case of the MCU, a single hero is not the entire system. Therefore, we must broaden our analysis to consider more than just one set of powers at a time. While the powers of each hero are rational, there is no logic, pattern, or thematic thread connecting all the heroes. Learning about Captain America in no way prepares us for Thor, just as Iron Man's abilities don't signal what the Hulk is capable of.

On a small scale, the magic system seems rational, but on a larger scale, it is not. If there were one or two power sets, an argument could be made that they are separate small magic systems. But by the time we get to *The Avengers*, we have four major heroes, a diabolical villain, and an invading alien race all with their own powers and abilities.

At this point, we can't consider them separate. How does the saying go? Two is a company and three is a crowd? Or is it three is a crowd and four is a party? Either way, we have so many unique magical powers that we need to consider them together. With that in mind, it's clear that the magic of the MCU is irrational in nature.

Stargate SG-1 (Rational Magic)

Since the magic system under consideration in *Stargate SG-1* is mostly technological in nature, it should come as no surprise that this is a rational magic system. Every gadget introduced has thought and rationality behind it. More than that, once a device is shown, we can extrapolate potential uses and quirks of the device. In fact, many episodes center on exploring exactly those facets of the technology introduced.

As for predicting what other technologies might exist, that's a little trickier. At first glance, the technology looks similar to the superpowers of the MCU, with each piece being distinct and unassociated from the rest. That is partly true and definitely brings the *Stargate SG-1* magic system closer to the irrational side of the axis.

But this is still a rational system because of the existence of an underlying connection among the technologies. Many of the devices are built to support one another, generating a more consistent pattern within the universe. For example, starships, hyperdrives, and inertial dampeners all come together to improve space travel and space combat.

What's more, all the devices require power of some kind, be it chemical, nuclear, or more advanced sources such as the Zero Point Modules (ZPMs). This makes all the technology feel like it belongs together, since a single source can power so many of the devices. Unlike the heroes in the MCU, this leads to a variety of magic effects that are truly a part of a singular system rather than several distinct ones.

How to Change It

Where a magic system sits along the rational/irrational axis comes down to creative problem-solving. When someone us, a character, a reader tries to use the magic in new or unintended ways, the attempt requires logic and reasoning. If that reasoning holds up and the attempt actually works, then the magic system becomes more rational. But if someone makes what seems to be a perfectly logical assumption and the attempt doesn't work, then the magic becomes more irrational.

Let's say that, in our system, whenever a magic-user summons fire, the air around them grows colder and frost forms on their clothing. The intended effect is obviously the production of fire, but the user sees a potential way to exploit this side effect. So they try to freeze a glass of water by producing a large flame in the other hand. If this experiment works, it tells us more about the magic system and shows us that it is rational.

Another place to start is the sensory cohesion of the system. As we describe the magic, or describe anything in writing, we want to engage the senses. What does the magic look like? How does it smell? Do different magical effects elicit specific emotions? Does the magic have a consistent taste? Is magic accompanied by some kind of tactile pressure, pain, or pleasure? Even if the effects are wildly different, if the magic produces similar sensory results, the magic system will feel more cohesive and therefore more rational.

For example, what if our magic system could summon an ally, harm an enemy, transmute matter, and allow the user to fly? These are wildly different effects, and it's difficult to imagine them being connected.

What if, however, whenever these effects were produced, the magic-user's skin expelled red mist and their mouth was filled with the taste of rotten peaches? Suddenly, there's a connection and similarity between summoning, harming, transmutation, and flight that didn't exist before. Our brains will automatically lump the magic together and assume there is some kind of explanation or pattern behind it all. Even if there isn't, it *feels* like there is, which makes the system more rational. If we go the opposite direction, turning every effect into a unique experience, the pieces of our system will become more irrational.

We can even pull a similar trick using thematic elements and motifs within the system. The magic in *Mistborn* takes advantage of this by connecting all the effects to metals. If our magic system centered on different types of wood, colors of light, triangles, body parts, or even just a sense of justice, it starts to feel like there has to be some kind of rational connection.

Adding thematic elements is often one of the easiest solutions for increasing the rationality of your magic system, as it rests entirely within description, narrative, and general flavor. Because these elements are contingent on the narrative and can vary wildly from system to system, *The Magic-System Blueprint* does not inherently capture these kinds of attributes, but there is a notes section at the end of the Blueprint where you can record and develop such ideas.

On a similar note, we can apply various patterns and structures to our magic system to generate an artificial system of logic and reasoning for the magic to follow. Rules like "X is always true except when Y happens" or "when the magic does X, Y also happens" make a magic system more rational. By definition, forcing the magic to adhere to such a structure makes it a more rational magic system.

Let's say that to heal an ally a magic-user says *corporis*, and then pinches their fingers together while whispering *simul*. There's a burst of wind, and the wounded flesh mends itself. We conclude that all magic is performed by speaking a material word, making a hand gesture, and speaking an action word. With this simple pattern in place, we can assume that, should they learn the appropriate material word, a magic-user could repair shattered wood, meld stone shards into a single piece, or fix a broken sword. We just made the system more rational.

Even with such structures in place, we can also shift the system in the opposite direction if we want. To make a system feel more irrational, we simply need to show that the logic doesn't work the same way all the time. By adding exceptions and contradictions, we make the logic chains of the system feel unreliable.

Even if we don't have a complete structure or pattern supporting our system, we can use rules and limitations to make it more rational or irrational. But simply having rules and limitations isn't enough. How they are built, defined, and explained will ultimately alter their rationality or irrationality.

As a rule of thumb, the more explicit and nuanced the rule or limitation, the more rational the magic system will feel.

Blueprint Connections

Hard/Soft Axis

The hard/soft axis is all about how much of the magic system we know and understand. Knowledge of a system illuminates patterns within that system, thus improving its odds of being a rational system.

This connection goes only one way. Just because we took the time to add nuanced rules and build in a strong theme doesn't suddenly mean we know more about the system. And it certainly doesn't mean other perspectives (readers, characters, etc.) will suddenly know more about the system.

Reliability

The rational/irrational axis connects to reliability in much the same way as the hard/soft axis does. When something is rational and predictable, we can better anticipate and trust that the magic will perform how we want it to. But there is limit to how much increasing the rationality of a system impacts the reliability.

Take a six-sided die with a number on each face ranging from one to six. Every roll gives us a one-in-six chance of rolling a specific number. And that's it. There's no amount of knowledge or rationality that will change the odds of us getting the exact number we want. The six-sided die is wholly rational, but it is not entirely reliable.

Naturalness

Higher levels of naturalness tend to lead to higher levels of rationality in a magic system. High levels of naturalness indicate that the natural creatures and phenomena of the world are linked or imbued with the magic. While nature can take some strange turns, much of what happens is, at least at some level, rational. That said, making a system more rational doesn't mean it becomes more natural as well. This is another one-way relationship.

Prevalence

Systems with higher prevalence often feel more rational. Even if there is no underlying pattern, people are pattern-seeking creatures and will create patterns where there are none, making the system feel more rational.

Consistency

If a system is consistent in thematic or sensory output, it will feel more rational. There doesn't actually have to be any pattern or rational explanation present, but the harmony will lead people to assume there is.

Types of Magic Outro

N ow that we've taken a look at both the hard/soft axis and the rational/irrational axis, it should be clear how closely the two spectra are linked. That leaves us with the grid found at the top of the Blueprint and four types of magic.

Hard-Rational Magic: The *majority* of the system is displayed or explained, and logic *can* be used to predict unseen portions of the system.

Hard-Irrational Magic: The *majority* of the system is displayed or explained, but logic *cannot* be used to predict unseen portions of the system.

Soft-Rational Magic: The *minority* of the system is displayed or explained, but logic *can* be used to predict unseen portions of the system.

Soft-Irrational Magic: The *minority* of the system is displayed or explained, and logic *cannot* be used to predict unseen portions of the system.

Examples

Mistborn (Hard-Rational Magic)

Allomancy from the *Mistborn* series is an exemplar of a hard-rational magic system. We learn most of the magic system early in the first book, *Mistborn: The Final Empire*. And once we learn those pieces, the system is rational enough that we can predict new applications of the magic.

All of this together is what makes Allomancy such a perfect example of a hard-rational magic system.

The Lord of the Rings (Soft-Irrational Magic)

As the readers and viewers, we see little magic throughout the series and learn even less about what it can do or how it works. And even when some magic is displayed, there is no way to accurately predict or theorize what might come next. There is no fundamental pattern to analyze. With that said, it should come as no surprise that the magic of *The Lord of the Rings* is a soft-irrational magic system.

Marvel Cinematic Universe (Hard-Irrational Magic)

The Marvel Cinematic Universe starts out small and grows larger as time goes on. Along every step of the way, we know the majority of what can and cannot happen in the system. The larger it grows, the softer it becomes, but as of the first *Avengers* movie, it is still a hard system.

At first glance, it appears to be rational as well. But as the system grows and we learn more, it becomes clear there are few patterns and themes that spread across the system as a whole. What we see in one movie with one hero tells us nothing about the next, making for an interesting irrational system.

Stargate SG-1 (Soft-Rational Magic)

From the very beginning, we understand that what we know and see as members of the audience is a tiny piece of a much larger universe. Even as we discover new technology and new capabilities, we know there is so much more out there waiting for us. That said, the pieces we have all behave in accordance with logic and reason. In fact, a major part of the show is using the rational nature of the magic to solve new and interesting problems.

Altogether, that makes the technology of *Stargate SG-1* a soft-rational magic system.

Last Remarks on the Types of Magic

As we've discussed in the last two chapters, where our system falls on the hard/soft and rational/irrational axes can have a big impact on our story. More than anything, the type of magic system we build will impact what we present to the readers and how we present it. The rest of the Blueprint helps nail down how our magic fits into the world, but identifying our magic in this way will heavily influence how the magic itself will feel to the audience.

Knowing the type of magic system we're building will determine how much we need to show, when to show it, and how much focus and emphasis to place on it. It will shape how we present the story and its tone. It will reveal how the readers feel while experiencing it.

Another important thing to note is that no one type of magic is better than the rest. Each type of magic system has its own strengths and weaknesses. It's all about how you use it.

Irrational magic systems are outstanding for horror and Lovecraftian stories where certain elements are meant to feel surprising, alien, and incomprehensible. They also provide the storyteller tremendous flexibility to make each magical-user or magical effect feel unique and the setting wild and uncharted. Softer magic systems are all but essential for any new-world or portal-fantasy story, as the characters seldom know anything about the magic in the beginning. Soft magic also heightens the sense of wonder and mystery while coaxing the reader to learn more. It's all about understanding the needs of the story and how the different types of magic can meet those needs.

I cannot stress this point enough, so I'm just going to say it again, but louder: no one type of magic is better than the rest!

One last thing: The exact placement of your system along the hard/soft and rational/irrational axes is up to you, but no matter where you place it, someone will disagree. That's normal. Everyone has a slightly different perspective. The important thing is that you identify your magic system in a way that helps you understand it and keeps you building your magic system and story.

Magic System Variables

L ET'S PAUSE for a moment to talk a bit more about how the Blueprint is divided up. So far, we have considered the name, the seed crystal of the system, the perspective taken while mapping the system, and what type of magic system it is.

The next portion of the Blueprint is dedicated to eight specific properties that identify how your magic functions within the world. These properties are called magic-system variables. Before getting into the details of each variable, we need to understand what they are and why they are important.

What Are Magic-System Variables?

Magic-system variables are the universal qualities of any magic system that we adjust and tweak to create something unique. I'm not talking about your magic effects or limitations here. Variables aren't a single idea or statement. Your magic-system variables control how the system is experienced from the chosen perspective. They're like the settings menu in a video game.

Whether it's *Skyrim*, *Borderlands*, or *Farmville*, there are a variety of options available to you as the player: screen brightness, color contrast, music and voice volume and balance, alternate controls. With few exceptions I'm looking at you, *Borderlands* you can even set the game difficulty to a level you can enjoy.

Separately, these game settings can seem insignificant. Taken as a whole, these settings have a massive impact on your enjoyment of the game and your play style. Just like the video game settings, your magic-system variables are more like a state of being that you can set rather than a single idea or statement.

Why Do Magic-System Variables Matter?

Magic-system variables matter because they *are* the system.

Just as the variables are more than a single idea or answer, a magic system is more than a cluster of disparate qualities. Your unique system results from these qualities acting together, blending and harmonizing into something unique and beautiful.

Now, on to the first variable!

Transference

What Is It?

Transference is all about how the magic effects and abilities are gained, lost, loaned, or stolen from a magic-user. Like most of the variables in the Blueprint, transference is a sliding scale from high to low. On the low end, it is extremely difficult, perhaps even impossible, to gain magical powers or control who has them. When transference is high, virtually anyone can easily acquire or receive the ability to perform magic.

The Details

When considering how to set this variable, it is important that you consider only the transference of magical ability and not the complexity of the ability itself.

For example, a magic sword, a personal computer, or even a cell phone can easily be handed off or picked up by anyone (transference). At this point, whoever possesses the object has access to the magic, but simply possessing the object doesn't guarantee they will have the skill or knowledge to use it (ease of use). So the magic can easily be transferred, but it might be difficult to use. How easy it is to actually produce or use the magical effect is another variable entirely (ease of use).

When we're exploring the transference of our magic system, we need to answer a couple of pivotal questions: How difficult is it to gain access to the magic? How easily can the power be stolen, purged, or otherwise lost? Is the magic innate in specific users, or can it be distributed at will throughout the population? Is it a matter of genetics (low transference), a complex but common ritual (medium transference), or just a matter of ownership (high transference)?

Another factor is whether the transference of power is permanent or temporary. With a technological device or magical artifact, all you really need is to possess the item. Superpowers and similar magic abilities are usually tied to one person and one person only. As a general rule, permanent abilities tend to have lower transference than temporary abilities.

Impact on Your Story

More than anything else, transference determines whether the system feels like traditional magic or like technology. Whether this is true technology functioning solely off scientific principles or a technology-like industry built around specific magical abilities, the system requires a high level of transference.

The transferability of a magic system will also impact the power dynamics within the world. We most commonly see this in systems where there is little to no way to control who gets and keeps the magic. In these cases, the magic-users are often at odds with those without magic. The magic-users want to make the most of their abilities, and those without are frightened of the power magic-users hold.

But this isn't the only power dynamic you can exploit. Perhaps magic-users are viewed as little more than batteries or power plants for society to run on. Even though they hold magical power, their social and economic power can be stripped away to place magic-users at a disadvantage. These kinds of power dynamics occur naturally, but transference can influence power dynamics in big ways.

Which brings us to our next point: how to apply pressure to characters.

Imagine this: Your characters are on a mission to prevent the launch of a nuclear missile. Their one hope relies on using some facet of the magic in the story to solve their problem. They have reached the climax, and the clock is ticking down. How the rest of this plays out depends on how the system is set up.

If there is little to no transference, then there is likely one, and only one, character capable of stopping the launch. Whether it's a unique biometric signature, magic computer-hacking abilities, or something else entirely, the success of the mission depends entirely on that character. The sole focus of the mission is to get that character in the right place, at the right time, and with the right kind of support in order to succeed.

Take the same situation and apply a magic system with a high degree of transference. The characters have discovered some master-bypass MacGuffin to cancel the launch. This may be an ancient artifact that will render the nuclear warhead inert or even a powerful weapon to shoot it out of the sky. Now, instead of success riding on a single person, the mission depends on getting a specific capability in the right place at the right time. The device can be handed off from person to person, stolen, lost, or duplicated to create the perfect story.

That's just one example. Different levels of transference allow us to apply pressure and find solutions in different ways.

Examples

Mistborn (Low Transference)

In the world of Scadrial, whether you have the power of Allomancy is mostly a matter of genetics. You are either born with it or you are not. Even among those born with this magic, most can burn one type of metal; they are referred to as Mistings. It is a rare gift indeed to be a full Mistborn with the ability to use all the metals. But even if you have the right blending of recessive genes, nobody simply has the ability from birth. To gain their power, every magic-user undergoes terrible trials and suffering that forces them to "snap" and unlock their latent abilities.

With few exceptions, you either have the power or you don't. There is no way to loan, borrow, or steal someone else's abilities without the intervention of a separate magic system. All of this combines to make a magic system with little to no transference.

The Lord of the Rings (Medium-Low Transference)

The magic in the *Lord of the Rings* series is a little tougher to analyze. From what we see, most magic is simply possessed by magical beings. Sauron, Galadriel, Gandalf, the Ents, and the elves are all innately magical beings. This would make it a low-transference system like Allomancy if it weren't for the Rings of Power. Many Rings of Power exist across Middle-earth, and we as the audience know precious little about them.

Most of the magic we see in the series centers on the One Ring. While the power in the One Ring originally came from the Dark Lord Sauron himself, it can be picked up and used by anyone. Granted, most use it to turn invisible, but there are many hints to the massive power it contains. Both Gandalf and Galadriel are afraid to even touch it, fearful of the power it contains.

While the magic of Middle-earth is likely a low-transference system, what the audience sees is more like a medium-low transference system.

Marvel Cinematic Universe (Medium-High Transference)

In the Marvel Cinematic Universe, we have a small number of individuals that have developed, found, or been granted their powers. At first glance, this might look like a low-transference system, but it actually falls closer to the middle of the spectrum.

Each hero is special, but their abilities don't have to remain unique to them. Iron Man is powerful because of the incredible suit and arc reactors he designed. Once created, anyone could take these tools and use them for themselves. In fact, replication and theft of Iron Man's technology is the focus of other Marvel movies. While it may be incredibly difficult to make an Iron Man suit, once it is created anyone can wear and use it.

This is true for more than just Iron Man. The serum used to create Captain America could be replicated, and any worthy individual can wield Thor's hammer. If we look past the MCU Phase One for just a moment, we can see that this pattern continues. The Black Panther gains his powers from the Heart-Shaped Herb. Anyone, including bad guys like Killmonger, can consume the herb and gain the same powers.

Overall, the MCU demonstrates a magic system with medium-high transference.

Stargate SG-1 (High Transference)

Stargate SG-1 is a perfect example of how high transference makes a system feel more like technology than magic. Throughout the series, we witness advanced cloaking effects, faster-than-light travel, regeneration capabilities, and even teleportation. None of these powers belong to any one person but are instead generated by objects and devices that can be used by anyone. In fact, most of the devices are designed with transportability and transference in mind.

How to Change It

Now that we have some solid examples in our brains, how can we twist and tweak a system to set the transference exactly where we want? Let's talk through some concepts.

First, let's look at how the power is gained in the first place. The more freely the magic can be picked up, and the more control users have over what they pick up, the greater the level of transference. In order to increase transference in our magic system, we need to make it easier to choose or control who does and does not have access to the magic.

Another method is to tamper with the permanence and longevity of the power. All other things being equal, a system with temporary magical effects and abilities will have higher transference than one with permanent effects and abilities. If the abilities are temporary, that means the powers can be lost. Whether the power is stripped away or simply fades over time, it's not guaranteed to be present forever.

We can also influence the transferability of a magic system by adjusting specific variables within the Blueprint.

If the source of magical power exists outside the character, we can create opportunities for the power to be tapped, discovered, or stolen by a wider range of characters. We can also decrease the prevalence of magic in the world by making it difficult to find and therefore difficult to obtain.

In my Viral Magic System, people gain magical powers when they are infected by a strain of magical virus. The magic lasts only as long as the virus is present in the body, and the magical effects are the strongest at the height of the illness. Once fully recovered, an individual is completely immune to the strain they contracted and cannot contract it again. That said, some of the viruses mutate rapidly like the real-world flu and can infect an otherwise immune individual. Lastly, the magical viruses behave like natural viruses and can easily infect others.

Altogether, this makes for a magic system with a high level of transference. So how exactly can we go about raising or lowering transference? Let's take another look.

Viruses are, by their nature, easily spread from one host to another. To further increase the transference of this system, we need to simplify the transference process or increase the level of control people have over it. The easiest way to do that would be to make the magical strains more common in the world. If the magic strains are easy to find, it is easier to become infected with the strain you want. This could mean going to the infectious disease ward of a hospital or even purchasing serums to infect yourself.

It's a little harder to decrease the transference of the Viral Magic System without violating the core principle of the system. Viruses are, by their nature, highly transferable. To change this, we would need to change the mechanisms by which the viruses themselves spread or how the power manifests.

Maybe the magical strains aren't transmitted through bodily fluids, but through combinations of ideas and emotions. One strain allows the user to disintegrate matter. Maybe that strain spreads only between people experiencing existential dread from the impermanence of all things. Quite specific and hard to replicate. It could be that the viruses are everywhere, but they become magical only when an infected user is exposed to a specific wavelength of light or radiation.

In another system, we might try making the transference and lending of power part of the system itself. Perhaps power (technological or magical) can be purchased or rented. Maybe magic-users routinely perform a ritual where they select exactly which powers they want for the coming days or months. It could even be as simple as going to a specific location and exposing yourself to a particular influence.

If we wanted to decrease the transference of a magic system, we simply do the opposite. Make the necessary ritual extremely dangerous and complex. Maybe the distribution or selection of magic-users is entirely arbitrary or occurs only in exceedingly strange situations. All these things will lower transference.

Blueprint Connections

Prevalence

If the magic system already meets a certain threshold of transference, then increasing prevalence will further increase the transference. If the power can already be gained and lost, like with the Viral Magic System, then making it easier to find will give potential magic-users greater access to the power.

Source

More often than not, a magic system with an external power source will have a higher level of transference than a system with an internal power source. If the power exists solely within the magic-user, that can be difficult to pull out and move to another. If the source is already external, then the system must already have a way for users to access the magic and manipulate it.

Rules and Limitations

These are not part of the Core Blueprint, but they are definitely related to transference because we can build rules and limitations by explicitly stating how power is lost, gained, or transferred. Rules and limitations can further define and explore how transference occurs, the complexity of such a process, and how much control a user might have over it.

Prevalence

What Is It?

Prevalence examines how widespread and commonplace the magic is from the chosen perspective. To set this variable properly, we need to ask the following:

* What percentage of the population has magical powers?

* Is magic something performed and witnessed every day or only once in a dozen lifetimes?

* Do magic-users exist evenly throughout the setting, or do certain areas contain more than others?

These kinds of questions pop up all the time when people discuss building magic systems. They are important, but I'm not happy leaving you with a couple of open-ended questions. So let's dig into the details of what prevalence is and how it works.

The Details

While we explore prevalence, it's vital that we establish our perspective and keep it in mind.

When adopting the perspective of our audience or our characters, it's straight-forward. With our audience, it's just a question of how much focus we want there to be on the magic in the story we're telling. Basically, how many words do we spend demonstrating or explaining the magic?

On a similar note, the prevalence from a character's perspective is all about what they see and how often they see it. If their life is overflowing with magic, then the prevalence is high. If they hardly see any magic, the prevalence is low.

This variable becomes more involved when exploring it from wider perspectives such as a person from a specific country, an entity from another world, or from our perspective as the creators.

First, we should consider the magic itself and all its various forms throughout the world. The setting may have lines of power that web across reality. Or maybe magic exists only around a specific location or phenomenon. Magical energies might swirl through the air, condensing into reality-warping clouds. Magic might be an anomaly that exists solely within the magic-users themselves and nowhere else in the universe.

We also need to consider the creatures and people capable of producing magical effects. Magic-users might belong to a single demographic or receive their magic through random assignment, or maybe magic lies dormant in everyone, just waiting to be harnessed. We must inspect the populations within the setting and decide how ubiquitous we want the magic to be within those boundaries.

And how do all these beings compare to one another? Maybe every magic-user has the same level of magical strength, and conflicts are determined by skill, creativity, and cunning. Conversely, magic-users may vary wildly in the strength of the magical effects they produce, and characters have to be careful to stay within their weight class. It could be that most people are about equal, with a few outliers that skew the system.

The decision is yours.

Next, let's consider some specific pieces of the magic system. Are all the abilities and effects the system offers spread evenly throughout the setting, or is it predisposed in some way? There might be effects and abilities seen everywhere, while a few special abilities appear only once in a hundred years.

Impact on Your Story

More than anything, prevalence affects how different characters will react when encountering the magic or magic-users. If it is something they see every day, they might ignore it completely. On the other hand, if they've never seen the magic before, they could respond with fear or wonder.

Then again, a character may be intimately familiar with the power they are witnessing and still have it scare them to death. The display may seem simple enough, but they have had enough experience to know how dangerous it can become.

The prevalence of the magic also impacts how readily characters can access the magic and how likely it is to appear in the story. This in turn determines what actions are available to them, where they can turn for help, what they can use to solve their problems, and so on.

In the case of prevalence, it's all about actions and reactions. We need to examine what reactions the characters have when using or witnessing the use of magic and how this guides their actions.

Examples

When it comes to analyzing magic systems from the audience's perspective, prevalence is a little different from the other variables. There are actually two perspectives to consider here. One is the prevalence of the magic in the story itself. Basically, how many pages in the book feature the magic? The other is how the reader interprets or evaluates the prevalence of the magic within the story setting as a whole.

Each section will contain a brief discussion of the prevalence of magic in the audience's experience, but we will focus primarily on the audience's evaluation of prevalence within the setting.

Mistborn (Medium-Low Prevalence)

From the perspective of the reader, the prevalence of magic is through the roof. Nearly all the point-of-view (POV) characters have access to Allomancy and use it liberally. The main characters fight in aerial battles, fling soldiers around, and unleash magical mayhem while fighting against equally powerful enemies.

But let's look at the audience's perceived prevalence of magic in the setting.

We know that Allomancy is a rare thing in the Final Empire, where the story takes place. The power primarily exists within the magic-users. Barring the gods themselves, there are no Allomantic powers in the natural spaces of the world, and most of the metals used to conduct Allomancy are not themselves magical.

What's more, the magic-users are not equally distributed across the empire. Luthadel, the empire's capital, contains the greatest concentration of Allomancers. This is partially due to politics but also because of the origin and transference of the magic. Allomancy is inherited through the noble bloodlines, and the Great Houses are the descendants of the Lord Ruler's closest friends.

The country nobles, therefore, have fewer Allomancers in their ranks, and the entire lower class of society is practically devoid of magic.

We also know that not all types of magic-users are as common as others. The Mistborn are powerful because they are rare and have access to all the powers, but Mistings have only one. This unbalances the playing field, but among magic-users with identical abilities, the power levels are fairly constant, though there are some outliers.

As a reader, all of this combines to make Allomancy a system with medium-low prevalence in the setting.

The Lord of the Rings (Low Prevalence)

The prevalence of magic in *The Lord of the Rings* is much easier to pin down.

As we watch the movies, we do experience and witness magic in the world. We know it's there, and we see a variety of magical races and a few magical effects. The plot pivots on one dangerously powerful magic item. Beyond that, very little of the magic in Middle-earth is ever explored or explained. We know certain objects and people have power, but there are no clues to the magnitude of this power or what they can do before they do it. We don't see much explicit use of the magic, but through the eyes of the audience, the magic is still somewhat prevalent.

Which is fascinating, because the perceived prevalence in the setting as a whole is quite different.

It could be argued that magic exists in the dragons, Ents, trolls, and other fantastical creatures of Middle-earth, though they don't have much in the way of magical abilities beyond simply existing. That said, beings with true magical powers do exist, but they are scattered throughout the various races, lands, and hidden places of the world. We know characters and forces with significant magical power exist, but such people are rare.

Much of the magic system in the *Lord of the Rings* series is a giant mystery and not just to us. It seems like most people living in Middle-earth can go their entire lives without encountering magical forces or beings. After looking at what we do know, it is clear that the magic is as scarce as it is varied, pointing toward a setting with a low prevalence of magic.

Marvel Cinematic Universe (Medium-Low Prevalence)

Much like with Mistborn, the audience experience is brimming with exposure to magical powers and magic-users. That's kind of the point. We watch the movies to see the epic struggles of equally epic magic-users, so the prevalence of magic in the experience itself has to be quite high.

But what about prevalence in the setting as a whole? That is, once again, a different story.

Most Marvel movies take place on Earth, in the modern day. Of course, there are extraordinary beings that possess various forms of magic, some human and some not. Either way, such beings are rare, one or two in a billion. On top of that, most of the heroes and villains are roughly on the same level of power, which leads to the epic and tense conflicts we know and love.

While there are variations in abilities and weaknesses between the heroes and villains, they all have a few things in common. For one, every character has access to some superhuman strength. On top of that, every hero gains exceptional resilience, allowing them to take a beating and get back up.

This leads to a system with medium-low prevalence. But given the strong positive flux of the universe, which we will discuss later, the prevalence might creep up a notch or two as more movies are added to the cinematic universe.

Stargate SG-1 (Medium Prevalence)

Once again, from the audience's perspective, the magic in the show is highly prevalent. It has to be. The Stargate itself is a critical component of the entire series, and not a single episode goes by where we don't witness this magic in action.

But in terms of the perceived prevalence of magic across the setting, the technology of *Stargate SG-1* strikes a fairly even balance.

All the "magical" technology and relics of the ancients and other races exist within the setting, simply waiting to be discovered. When humanity enters the universe at large, there are all kinds of natural powers and phenomena floating around them.

The prevalence and power of the individual pieces of technology vary wildly. The scarcity of powerful technology, at least for the humans from the Milky Way, known to others as the Tau'ri, is a big part of the plot. Common technology in *Stargate SG-1* is comparable to technology we have in the real world, such as guns and ships, even if they are far superior.

Combine all that together and we have a system that sits comfortably in the middle of the prevalence spectrum.

How to Change It

Ultimately, changing prevalence comes down to decision and clarification. Pick where you want it, and make sure you have an idea as to why it is the way it is.

It could be that, in the previous age, all magic-users were hunted down and put to death. Now only a few people in a generation have the right mix of genetics to access the ancient powers. You could limit the magic to a specific gender, age group, nationality, or even hair color. In the end, it's just a matter of how you explain it.

That said, one easy way to increase the prevalence of a magic system is to make it function like technology. The fact that it is understood enough to mass-produce, or at least consistently reproduce, will lead to greater availability of the magic and greater likelihood that people will encounter it in their day-to-day lives.

If you're exploring prevalence from the perspective of a reader, protagonist, or character, it's all about exposure and the picture we want to paint for them. The more magic encountered through a given perspective heightens the prevalence of magic. Combined with what they know about the rest of the system and setting as a whole, this will shape their understanding and view of how common magic is on a larger scale.

For my Viral Magic System, I built the magic system for a story in which the magical viruses are quite new to the world. People know they exist and cause mayhem where they appear, but also that the viruses are uncommon. As a character, you would have a hard time hunting down a specific strain. Overall, I was shooting for a medium-low prevalence.

Changing that would be pretty easy to do. To increase the prevalence, I could make the strains more infectious. The world could face a pandemic of these magical strains, making it easier to get infected. With access to infectious disease wards, a character could identify patients and expose themselves to exactly the strain they desired.

To lower the prevalence, I could dial back the infection rate of the strains, or just roll back the clock on my timeline. If the story takes place closer to when the viruses first appear, they will be even less common. Over time the diseases would spread, but for the snapshot of a single story or two, I could make the prevalence as low as I want.

I could also introduce similar magical strains in different animal populations across the globe, maybe even create viruses that affect plants. Imagine a forest blight that produces magical effects as it grows in strength and spreads from tree to tree. There could be all kinds of reality-warping or deleterious effects generated by the dying trees, which would make for a fascinating setting.

You know what? That's supercool. Pardon me while I go write that down.

Blueprint Connections

Perspective

Prevalence won't seem the same to all people. Even in the examples covered earlier, we identified two different assessments for each system while solely in the perspective of the audience.

Hard/Soft Axis

All things being equal, greater prevalence tends to a harder magic system. If people see magic regularly, they will likely know and understand more about it. The more they see, the harder the system becomes to them. This is true both for characters and for the audience.

Rational/Irrational Axis

The more common the magic, the more likely people are to encounter it, and as they encounter it, they have a greater chance of establishing patterns, thus rationalizing the system. These patterns may not actually be true, but humans generate false patterns all the time to better understand and comprehend the world around them.

Flux

In many ways, the flux of a magic system measures the rate at which the prevalence is changing over time. If the flux is positive, the prevalence of magic is going up. Negative flux leads to a decrease of prevalence over time, and neutral flux means no change is occurring in either direction. While flux can, and often will, change the prevalence of the system, prevalence does not affect flux in turn.

Transference

If there is a certain level of active transference occurring within a magic system, then the prevalence of the magic can drive it further in either direction. If magic can be handed from one person to another, then the more magic there is in the world, and the more likely these types of exchanges will occur. Lowering prevalence makes it more difficult for someone to find a source of power and complete the desired transfer.

Source

What Is It?

Source is the power within a magic system and where it comes from, how much is present, and whether it can run out or be renewed. It's all about examining the flow of power from its core to the production of a magical effect.

Many of the variables on the Blueprint exist as sliding scales, but the source variable is a little different. Instead of a single scale, it has two distinct attributes, each with a limited number of options. Those two attributes are where the magic comes from relative to the magic-user and how much energy is available.

The Details

First, regarding the origin of magic, it can come from inside the user (internal source) or from outside the user (external source). Internal sources are commonly found in traditional magic systems. The power fueling the magic is generated and stored somewhere inside the magic-user, or the user is part the system or source itself. With external sources, the power used to produce magical effects is generated or fueled by a specific thing from outside the user. As such, external sources are more common in technological magic systems, where external tools laser pistols, mini atomic reactors, hyperdrive produce the effects rather than the people themselves.

When a source is tapped to produce a magical effect, this can have a direct impact on the source. It all depends on how the energy is generated and how the pool of energy functions. Internal and external sources can be finite, infinite, or renewable.

With an infinite source, the magic-user can tap into the source of their magic forever without it faltering or stopping. If a magic-user can access their power without concern for materials, exhaustion, or anything else, then it is an infinite source. These can be tricky to spot at times, because a system with an infinite source may not seem to have a source at all. Because it's never at risk and never changing, the story might not even mention the source. But even if the type of source is never discussed, an infinite source is still there, fueling the magical effects.

A finite source is, naturally, the opposite. The magical source has limited pool of power that fuels the magical effects. In such cases, the size of the source, the rate at which the source is drained, and what happens when it runs out are all important factors for the magic-user and us, as creators to consider. A user with a massive energy source can maintain a steady flow of magic for hours. Another might have enough energy to maintain a flow for only a few seconds.

There is one other extremely important factor for a finite source. Once the magical energy is consumed, there is no replacing it. When a finite source of power runs out, it becomes dead and can no longer fuel any effects or powers. If we want the source to run dry temporarily, that's where renewable sources come into play.

A renewable source functions similarly to a finite source, where power is consumed as magical effects are produced. But while finite sources are simply used until they are empty, renewable sources have some way of being replenished. The source could regain power passively over time. In other cases, specific actions, materials, or events may be required to refill the source. That means a renewable source can run dry, preventing further use of magic, but it won't stay dry forever.

As with so much of the magic-building process, how we decide to replenish a renewable source is up to us. Time is a common mode of replenishment. We can also introduce a specific fuel that must be gathered and used to generate any kind of magical effect. We can even do a combination of both, where the source can renew with time but some materials jump-start the process. That's right. We just added mana potions into the system. You're welcome . . . I think.

Some magic systems can have more than one source. This is most common in systems comprised of many disparate and unique abilities. When building a magic system with multiple sources of power, be sure to identify the location and nature of each source.

Finally, when exploring the source of a magic system, we need to examine the right concepts. Source determines where the energy comes from, how the energy flows, and the energy reserve itself, but it is not necessarily the thing that granted the user their power in the first place.

For example, just because a magic-user is born with the ability to perform magic doesn't mean the source of that magic is internal. The source could come from an external well of power (enchanted amulet), a preexisting network (hidden ley lines), or even another entity (a devil with a signed contract).

Impact on Your Story

When we modify the magic source for a system, the few effects those changes have on the story mostly involve how the characters behave and what their options are.

The type of source can enhance or limit a character's access to the magic, which will drive how often the magic is used, how it is used, how an antagonist responds to the protagonist's magic, what situations a character is best suited to handle, and more. Mostly it affects their behavior and the decisions they must make when using the magic.

If a magic-user knows the source is finite, they will likely hold their powers in reserve, using them only as a last resort. Infinite sources provide the user the greatest amount of flexibility and leeway to use their powers as they see fit. Renewable sources take a little from both, with the added complication that magic-users must always have a plan for refilling their reserves.

As for indirect impact, the source of a magic system often affects our world-building efforts. If the source of magic is external to the magic-users, then where is it? Where does it come from? Is it in the same place all the time, or does it move around? Can it be tracked or predicted? All these questions will impact where settlements arise, how much they grow, and what the people in them focus their attention on.

Examples

Mistborn (External and Renewable Sources)

The magical source for Allomancy is an interesting case study. In order to produce magical effects, three things must happen. First, a magic-user must obtain the metal associated with a specific effect. Second, the magic-user must then swallow the metal. Finally, the magic-user "burns" the metal within them, generating the magical effect and consuming the metal in the process. Once they burn through all their metal, they must obtain and consume more before generating further magical effects.

Through these three steps, it is abundantly clear from our perspective as the reader, and likely from the perspective of the characters, that the source of Allomancy is renewable. The magic consumes the reserve of power as the effects are produced, and once the reserve runs out, the magic stops. The magic-user need only obtain and swallow more metal, and just like that their reserves are renewed.

In this particular case, the perspective is important. With the limited scope we have as readers, we don't know what exactly is happening to the metal when it is "burned." It could be that the matter is completely destroyed. On the one hand, on a global or universal level, metal is a finite material. Eventually, it is possible for all metal to be burned by Allomancers and disappear from the world of Scadrial entirely. On the other hand, over the course of the series, we learn that God Metals regrow. This might be true for all metal in the *Mistborn* series, in which case it is truly renewable, even from the wider perspective. But we don't know for sure, and from the limits of what we see in the books, the power is renewable on a user-by-user basis.

Determining whether the magic of Allomancy has an internal or an external power source is a bit trickier. That's because the metals used by magic-users act as an external fuel but are then burned for power inside the user. Arguments can be made either way, but I believe the source is external. No magic can occur without the metal. No metal means no power. On top of that, the metal itself is something the magic-user must collect. We know that people have trace amounts of metal in their blood, bones, and tissue, but Allomancers seem to burn only the metal within their stomachs to generate magical effects. It might be possible to do otherwise, but because it is never shown, we cannot be sure.

All of this combines into a magic system with an external and renewable power source.

The Lord of the Rings (External and Infinite)

The softness of the magic in *The Lord of the Rings* makes analysis difficult. So little of the magic is shown that we can only guess at how it works and what it can do. But there are a few things we do know.

First, the One Ring contains the power of the Dark Lord Sauron, and the ring then grants a sliver of this power to the wearer to turn them invisible. Second, Gandalf's magic has some kind of connection to his staff. When his staff is taken away or destroyed, Gandalf seems to lose much of his ability to produce magical effects. Third, the light of Eärendil is contained within a phial and can be handed off to a wayward hobbit in way over his head.

Beyond that, we don't witness much magic. We know there are individuals that possess power, but it is unclear how the energy flows to produce the magical effects. Which is why, from our perspective in the audience, the magic system seems to have external power sources, not internal ones. With more knowledge from other works by Tolkien, we may learn the magic is actually internal, but we are limited in what we see and know, which leaves us with an external source.

The second attribute is much easier to identify. Throughout the story, there is never a concern of the power draining from the One Ring, Gandalf's staff, or any of the other magical items. None of the magic-users ever express concern about running dry on power or exhausting themselves. In fact, if the reserves could be depleted, then our heroes might have used an entirely different approach to destroying the One Ring. As it stands, the magical reserves always seem to be present, simply waiting to be used as much or as little as desired.

Put that together and you have an infinite, external sources of magic.

Marvel Cinematic Universe (Infinite, Internal and External)

Many magic systems stick to a single source of power, but the Marvel Cinematic Universe switches it up a bit between the characters. Some of the magic sources within the MCU are internal and some are external. Let's take a closer look at the original Avengers.

Tony Stark's superpower is, arguably, his incredible intelligence, but his actual magical powers come from his iconic suit of armor and the other technology he creates. Once developed, his devices can be taken away and used by anyone (transference). More importantly, he can't use any of his abilities without his tech, making the source of his powers decidedly external.

Thor is in a similar position. From the perspective of the audience, Thor's power comes from his hammer, Mjolnir. In fact, that's the entire plot of the first *Thor* movie. He has been separated from the source of his power and must prove his worth once again. Now the nature of Thor's source can, and does, change in future movies, but as of the first *Avengers* movie, this is another external power source.

Now, what do Captain America and the Incredible Hulk have in common? Well, they both have internal power sources. In both cases, all strength and abilities they have are part of them and their bodies. The Hulk doesn't draw power from radiation, and Captain America doesn't need his shield in order to be amazing. The origin of their powers and how they were transferred to them are different, but both clearly have internal power sources.

Regardless of the character in question, all the magic sources in the MCU have one thing in common: they are all infinite. With the exception of Iron Man in the first movie, we never experience the magic-users running out of magical energy or power. Loki can always create his illusions, the Hulk's strength never flags, and Thor always has more lightning. Every magic-user and every source they tap has an infinite supply of power.

Overall, the MCU gives us a mixture of internal and external energy sources, but all of them are infinite.

Stargate SG-1 (External and Renewable)

Before digging into this example, it is important to remember perspective when analyzing it. Our discussions of the magic in *Stargate SG-1* have focused exclusively on the technology shared by the races and not the racial abilities they possess.

With that in mind, it should be no surprise that the technology serves as an external source of magic. This is one of the distinctive traits of any technological magic system. It is the technology itself, and not the individual holding it, that provides the power.

The nature of the power reserves is also fairly straightforward. Engines, weapons, and other devices can all run out of power. Once the power is gone, any effects they produce stop. From what is seen in the series, most of these reserves either refill with time or are easily replaced. Running out of power to activate a shield, maintain a cloaking device, or fire a weapon is usually only an issue for an episode or two. After that, the characters find a way to make the technology functional again.

Put it together and the magic system in *Stargate SG-1* clearly functions because of external, renewable sources of power.

How to Change It

To make a source external, take the well of power that originally existed within the magic-user and place the power within a device, charm, or piece of special material instead. As long as the character is in possession of the thing, they have access to the unending power; take it away and they lose everything. Just like that, the internal source is now an external one. If we flip the process, taking the source from the thing and placing it inside the magic-user, we've turned an external source into an internal one.

We can also change whether a source is internal or external by introducing new information or presenting the system from a new angle. The characters might think their magic is purely internal, right up until something severs their connection to the source. Suddenly, they are confused and unable to access any of their magic. In a similar fashion, a character may spend some time believing their power comes from some special place or thing only to learn the true source is within themselves.

But just because a source is external does not mean anyone can use it. Whether others can pick up and use the magic is a factor of transference. A magical power source can be external and exclusive to any magic-users, or even a specific magic-user. Remember when we talked about Allomancy? The metals are external to the magic-user, and any user can consume them to power their own abilities. But swallowing metal doesn't suddenly turn a normal person into a magic-user.

Depending on perspective, the lines between an infinite, finite, and renewable power source can get fuzzy at times, and you can use that to your advantage when crafting your story. From the perspective of a character or an audience, it's all about what they see and the knowledge they have. A power source may seem infinite right up until the energy reserve runs dry. At that moment, the magic-user or the audience might assume it has been depleted forever until they experience the energy return or discover a way to make it return.

As the creators of the system and authors of the story, it is up to us to communicate what the power source is to our characters and our readers alike.

In the Viral Magic System, all magical effects come from the viruses themselves. A person does not have the magic without being infected by the virus, and the strength of their magical effects is dependent on the number of virions (virus particles) present in their body. The magic is a persistent effect generated by the virions themselves and endures as long as the virions are still viable.

Together, this system has an infinite, external power source, even though that external source exists inside the host's body.

If we wanted to change the source from external to internal, we need to shift the energy source from the virions to the host. The virus could simply act as the catalyst and origin of the magic, infecting the host and unleashing magical powers within. In this case, the actual power comes from the host themselves. We could also blur the lines between internal and external even more. Maybe the virus still generates the power, but it needs something special from the host's body in order to do so. Now something in the host is acting as fuel for the whole process. In this case, it could feel more internal or external depending on how we portray it in the story.

But what if we want to make the infinite source of the Viral Magic into a finite or renewable source? To make this work, we need to understand the size of the energy pool, how quickly it drains, and what happens when it runs out.

The size and speed at which the magic drains could be dependent on the individual strain, but what happens when it runs out? Maybe overusing the magic drains energy from the virions themselves. If the user overdraws on the magic, they could completely destroy the viral infection, which is good if you're tired of being sick, but bad if you still need the power. It could also be that using the magic fuels virus mutation. The power runs out when the relevant strain has completely mutated into something new. At that point, the host may have a new power or become patient zero of the world's deadliest disease.

Once we have the details of how it works as a finite source, turning it into a renewable source is a snap. We just have to generate some way to refill the well of power or prevent the source from running dry in the first place. Special antiviral medication could slow or kill the new strain as it appears. You could introduce something special that the virus uses to recharge itself, such as a basic nutrient or an extraordinary substance. It could even be that the virus regenerates its power when the host infects someone new.

Let's say we're looking at a different system altogether. We have an internal and renewable magic source we want to make external. We simply make the source into a well of power somewhere in the world that the character must return to time and again to recharge their abilities. If the character runs out of strength, they can return to the well and draw from what could easily be an infinite, finite, or renewable source of its own.

There are so many ways we can do this. While changing the nature of the source is simple, it can have a massive impact on the balance of the system.

The source is a huge factor in how magic-users behave and utilize their magic. If you change the nature of your source, be sure to retest the system for any newly formed cracks and loopholes.

Blueprint Connections

Perspective

The angle from which we observe the magic will dictate how the source appears to function. What seems like a finite source from the perspective of a magic-user might actually be renewable in the grand scheme of things.

Hard/Soft Axis

Depending on where a magic source falls on the hard/soft axis, as in what knowledge and understanding is available to a given perspective, that source may seem finite, infinite, or renewable when, in truth, it is something else altogether.

Transference

External sources are generally easier to give, take, or move around, while internal sources tend to have lower transference.

Transference and source can sometimes masquerade as each other. The origin of the magic, where the ability itself comes from, is a factor of transference and not source. You can have an external origin that leads to an internal power source. Just look at Captain America. His abilities came from a special serum (external), but once the serum is administered to him, his powers all exist within him and are fueled internally.

Flux

The flux of magic in your world is unlikely to affect whether a magical source is internal or external. It will, however, have direct connections to the type of reserve. If the source is finite, then using the magic forever diminishes the source, creating an instance of negative flux. Renewable and infinite sources are more likely to result in neutral flux than positive or negative flux.

This can easily be modified or countered with tweaks to the system, the world, the characters, and especially the perspective. For example, you can set the flux of the world or universe to be whatever you want, and the individual magic-user is unlikely to notice. They will see only that their personal source doesn't change or refill easily. They might also miss the changes occurring on a larger scale.

Ease of Use

Magic systems with internal sources of power are easier to use than those with external sources of power. It's a simple matter of access. If the magic is always present, that is one less thing for the user to think about and manage. It's simply there.

And, all other things being equal, making the magic source renewable or finite complicates the process of using the magic. Now, in addition to simply activating the magic, the magic-user must monitor and manage their magical reserves lest they run out when they need them most. Efficiency and planning for how to renew a power reserve become important considerations, making the process more difficult to manage.

Flux

What Is It?

Flux is the rate at which the magic within a defined boundary changes over time. If the amount of magic within the defined region increases, then the flux is positive; if the amount decreases, then the flux is negative. In cases where the magic doesn't change, whether because it is purely static or because the amount entering equals the amount leaving, the flux is neutral.

The Details

Flux is intrinsically tied to prevalence. In fact, it might be easier to think of flux as the rate at which the prevalence of a magic system changes, similar to how acceleration measures the rate of change in an object's speed.

While we could try to quantify the flux of a magic system, that is not what makes this variable useful. It is most helpful to magic-builders when used as a simple marker of how things are changing. With that in mind, there are three forms of flux any magic system can experience: positive, negative, and neutral.

Positive flux means that more magic is entering the system than is leaving. The nature of this change will vary depending on the perspective adopted while mapping the system. It could signify the birth of magic in a world, its development and growth. If perspective is limited to a single character, the flux could represent the change in their personal power. Whatever it is, the amount of magic added to the system is greater than the amount leaving.

If more magic is leaving the system than is entering, then the magic is in a state of negative flux. Again, exactly what this means depends entirely on the perspective we have set. The magic of the world could be disappearing, consumed by mankind's endless consumption of power. It could even signify a hero's magical potency decreasing over the years. The specifics are entirely up to you.

In a state of neutral flux, there is no change happening to the overall prevalence of magic from the defined perspective. This doesn't mean the system isn't changing; magic can still be leaving or entering. Regardless of the specific scenario, if the amount of magic leaving equals the amount entering, the system remains in a net neutral state.

Impact on Your Story

While other variables tell you how the magic looks, feels, or behaves right now, flux tells you how it will behave in the future and how it behaved in the past. Although flux won't have a large impact on any scene in a story, it can drastically change things during the world-building process or over the course of the story or series.

Audiences don't want everything in a story to stay the same forever. Change is interesting and fun. By modifying the flux of magic in your world, you can create a variety of arcs for the magic, the characters, and the world itself.

Writing a grimdark series about the loss of hope and rebirth of identity? Have the world start with a strong presence of magic that fades away a bit at a time. The characters, once so powerful and capable, are now just ordinary people brought low by struggles they never had to face before. And when the magic disappears entirely, the characters, and the world as a whole, will need to redefine and rebuild themselves in order to survive.

If you want to bring about a literal and metaphorical changing of the guard, flux can help with that too. Slowly fade out one aspect of the magic while another grows in its place. The setting and the characters are never without magic (neutral flux), but the nature of the magic can change drastically. Keeping the total system balanced while shifting other pieces in and out can lead to fascinating conflicts and character moments.

A magic system can always serve as a foil and augmentation for various aspects of your story. Clever manipulation and application of a system's flux allows you to make the same enhancements on a larger scale.

Examples

Mistborn (Neutral Flux)

As readers observing the world as a whole, the magic of Allomancy from the *Mistborn* series is an outstanding example of a system with neutral flux.

On a macro level, the amount of power in the world is constant and unchanging. At first, the flux may seem negative: magic-users consume metal, a finite source, to create magic.

Except we aren't concerned with just the metals. We're looking at the magic.

Flux needs to consider the prevalence and power of the magic as well as the source. In the series, the number of magic-users continues to increase with each generation, but their powers weaken. This is a perfect example of the nature of the magic changing while the flux remains neutral. And at the very end of the series, we learn that the power generating and fueling Allomancy cannot truly be destroyed, only transferred and transformed.

Allomancy even has neutral flux on a user level. Over time, magic-users consume metals (positive flux) and then burn them away (negative flux) to generate magical effects. The two actions balance each other out. On top of that, a magic-user's inherent power, once unlocked, never grows or fades. That's why this system has an overall neutral flux.

The Lord of the Rings (Negative Flux)

Magic is fading from Middle-earth. It's right in the intro of the first movie, when Galadriel says, "Much that once was is lost, for none now live who remember it."

While magic can be found hidden away in most corners of the world, this changes as the story unfolds. By the end, Saruman the White is killed, the One Ring is destroyed, and the Dark Lord Sauron is defeated. Three major sources of power, albeit evil ones, have disappeared from the world. But that's not the only change happening.

The Ents are dying out. With the loss of the Entwives, it's only a matter of time before they fade away into history. On top of that, the elves are setting sail for the west. And if that wasn't enough, all the ring bearers are going with them.

By the end of the series, the world of Middle-earth is less magical than it was before, which is why *The Lord of the Rings* is a perfect example of a magic system with negative flux.

Marvel Cinematic Universe (Positive Flux)

With each passing Marvel movie, more extraordinary beings appear in the world. The MCU continues to grow in scope and in danger as the audience sees new worlds, villains, and heroes. The cataclysmic events grow in scope and frequency as time goes on. In the first movies, the conflict is limited to terrestrial powers, but by the time *The Avengers* comes along, the conflict has gone extraterrestrial. Even on an individual level, most of the heroes continue to grow in power as they learn and develop.

However we want to look at it, this is a textbook example of positive flux.

Stargate SG-1 (Positive Flux)

The amount of advanced technology, as well as users with advanced knowledge of this advanced technology, steadily increases over the course of the series. All the races grow and change in their technical capabilities, but humanity experiences this the strongest. And it's not just a matter of rediscovering old technology that already exists if it were that, the magic system might have neutral flux instead. As the races learn and grow, they develop new forms and iterations of the various technologies.

This is another excellent example of a magic system and setting with positive flux.

How to Change It

As stated before, changing the nature of flux is a matter of perspective. Who is observing the flux?

If we consider things from a character level, an injury could permanently damage their ability to perform magic. Or perhaps they have unlocked new potential, experiencing a massive positive flux in their lives. Skills can be forgotten, abilities diminished, and minds broken.

If we consider state of flux for an entire world, our methods don't need to be epic. Certainly, the entire world could be running dry of magical energy, or more energy could pour through a massive rent in the fabric of the universe. World-level flux can consist of smaller levels of flux happening thousands of times. Look at what we did to create a state of flux for a specific character. What if that same thing were happening to every magic-user in the setting?

If we want to achieve a state of neutral flux, the simplest answer is to keep things the same. No change means no flux. But we can also take our favorite changes from both the positive and negative sides of the equation so they cancel each other out. As long as the two balance, the flux remains neutral. Entire magic systems could fade and be replaced while the setting maintains a state of neutral flux.

When we revisit the Viral Magic System, it's pretty clear that system has positive flux. The setting was mundane until the strains of magical viruses started appearing. That transition from no magic to any amount of magic is positive flux. And the flux will remain positive as new strains appear, spread, and mutate.

To make the flux negative, the proliferation of magical viruses would need to decline. High-enough mortality rates could also cause negative flux, so long as more hosts (magic-users) are dying than are infected.

Setting the Viral Magic System to neutral? That's tricky.

The easiest solution is to stabilize the world and report no noticeable increase or decrease in cases of the magical diseases. We could also broaden the perspective to include all magic systems in the world and not just the Viral Magic System. If that were the case, the viruses might kill off all magic-users of another type of system while creating new types of magic-users in their stead. This exchange could also happen on a viral level, where one strain fades as another replaces it. All these solutions would require more explanation and exploration of the setting, but they would ultimately result in neutral flux.

As you can see, there are lots of options here. How you go about this for your magic system is entirely up to you.

Blueprint Connections

Perspective

While the perspective impacts most variables on the Blueprint, its influence on flux is especially pronounced. Remember, flux is defined as the rate at which magical prevalence changes *within a defined area*. Your perspective determines that area.

Shifting perspective from a universal view to a national, regional, or even individual view might change what kind of flux is experienced. Beyond that, we can narrow the focus as much as we like. There are times where it's beneficial to map a system from the perspective of a single character. In that case, the flux would measure the growth or decay of magical ability for that specific magic-user.

Prevalence

Flux measures the change in prevalence over time. As long as magic is present somewhere in your story, you need to consider flux. In order for prevalence to change, the flux must be positive or negative. In that respect, flux has a far greater impact on prevalence than prevalence does on flux. Even if the story starts with no magic whatsoever, shifting from absolutely no magic (zero prevalence) to the tiniest bit of magic (low prevalence) requires positive flux.

Source

Certain types of magical sources lend themselves well to certain types of flux. A finite source of magic, where magic is performed and drained away, will likely experience negative flux. Renewable sources, like we see with Allomancy, will have moments of positive flux and negative flux, which then lead to an overall neutral state. Infinite sources, depending on the perspective, are the source most likely to experience positive flux. They cannot run out, so the measurable amount of magic can simply keep increasing.

Naturalness

What Is It?

Naturalness is how "natural" the magic is compared to the rest of the setting around it. Systems with high naturalness feel like a smooth extension of the setting, often blending with other wondrous or strange elements until they are difficult to separate from each other. Systems with low naturalness can feel like a bizarre, aberrant, or otherworldly addition to the setting. Other times they feel familiar, but they stand out strongly from the setting around them.

The Details

What makes a magic system feel normal or natural?

Sometimes it's obvious. The effects in a system with high naturalness may feel integrated with the natural laws, connected with the wildlife, and generally like an extension of the environment. Systems on the low end of the naturalness scale are often jarring deviations from everything else. They ignore established laws of nature and don't match the rest of the setting.

Let's say a character in our world taps into their magic. They find they can manipulate weather patterns and suddenly understand the universal language of beasts. This feels natural. A little strange and new for us and the character, but the magic seems to provide a deeper connection to the setting and the various forms of life within it.

Now imagine that a spaceship suddenly arrives in Earth's atmosphere. The character must now face shape-shifting aliens with the ability to control the minds of man. The magic possessed by the aliens is less natural to the characters than speaking with animals. Closer inspection may reveal these magic effects are connected, but shape-shifting mind-control aliens will initially seem to have little resonance with the rest of the setting we know.

Once again, perspective makes a huge difference here. What feels natural from one frame of reference won't feel that way from another. Even though naturalness is closely tied to perspective, we can shape the naturalness of a magic system in more objective ways.

One such area is the natural laws of the setting. More specifically, how well does the magic match said natural laws?

Bear in mind, the natural laws of the setting may be very different from those on Earth. Naturalness is about how the magic compares to everything around it, not how it compares to our world. Therefore, if the magic adheres strongly to the natural laws of the setting, it will feel like it belongs there and contribute to a greater sense of naturalness.

Take the concept a little further and we can examine the existence or absence of magic in nature. How much magic appears in the wild, if any at all? Maybe creatures in the setting have access to some of or all the magic system. Magic might saturate certain areas, spontaneously producing magical effects. Creatures, landmarks, natural materials, weather patterns, and natural disasters can all be pieces of the magic system. The more the magic appears in the setting beyond the influence of magic-users, the higher the naturalness of the system.

Impact on Your Story

Ultimately, naturalness is a matter of flavor and presentation. Through description, explanation, and other techniques, any system can feel like a natural part of the world around it. On the same note, even the most natural things can be twisted into something otherworldly, disjointed, and disconnected from reality.

These kinds of changes will have the greatest impact on the hearts and minds of the characters themselves. How will they react to seeing it? What scares them? What slips by their notice, and what sticks out like a glowing neon sign in a swamp?

We can extend this further to world-building, which will reflect the magical nature of the setting in the culture and habits developed by people and animals. If the magic is woven into daily rituals and skill sets of professional workers, this will support a system with high naturalness. An area in the wilds filled with so much malevolence that even insects avoid it would feel unsettling, out of place, and unnatural.

Naturalness can also have an enormous impact on the theme and tone of the story. Industrialization is a major theme in *The Lord of the Rings*, and Tolkien emphasized it by juxtaposing the orcs and dark lands of Mordor against the natural magic of Middle-earth.

Speaking of *The Lord of the Rings*, let's look at our example systems for a better idea on how naturalness can manifest within a story.

Examples

Mistborn (Medium Naturalness)

Throughout the entire series, Allomancy is only ever used by humans or creatures who were once human. There are no predatory animals enhancing their senses by burning tin or scavengers calming the emotions of other creatures around them (though that would be unbelievably cool). The magic never manifests in the setting outside human magic-users. There are no magical storms or magical forces of nature experienced in the story.

Later in the series, we learn that the power of Allomancy was granted to humanity by godlike entities who created the world. For some, this likely makes the magic feel more natural and connected to the setting, but because we don't know how natural the gods are, I don't think it influences the naturalness of the system at all.

The magic does follow the natural laws of the setting rather well. Steel-Pushing and Iron-Pulling (telekinetically moving metal toward or away from the magic-user) are both deeply rooted in the laws of physics. There are places where it deviates, but those deviations are fairly intuitive and easy to follow.

The system does, however, have its quirks. Tin, for example, can enhance all the human senses at once. This ability is primarily used to see through the dense mists blanketing the Final Empire at night. This seems to make sense at first, but as one character learns later in the series, it actually doesn't. Simply increasing the light sensitivity of the eye wouldn't make it easier to see through mist. Quite the opposite, in fact.

In this case, the magic starts seeming fairly natural, but when this tidbit is revealed, it lowers the naturalness of the system. Suddenly it doesn't feel as rooted in and connected to the world around it. When considering all the various quirks and facets of the magic system, Allomancy sits firmly in the middle of the naturalness spectrum.

The Lord of the Rings (High Naturalness)

The magic of Middle-earth might not be common, but it is deeply embedded in the setting around it. There are several kinds of wondrous and magical creatures that are a natural, if somewhat uncommon, part of the environment. Wargs, dragons, Ents, and trolls exist beyond the meddling or power of man, elves, wizards, or dark lords. What magic we do see shows no evidence of contradicting itself or the rest of nature. Even the magic-users fit neatly into the setting. They feel no more out of place than a rare gem.

Therefore, it should be no surprise that this magic system sits high on the spectrum of naturalness.

Marvel Cinematic Universe (Low Naturalness)

Let's talk this through.

We don't see the magic of the MCU anywhere outside the extraordinary beings and their incredible abilities. On top of that, their abilities often contradict or ignore the natural laws of our world.

It's a little different if we consider things from the Asgardian perspective. But even in Asgard, people with the powers of Thor, Loki, or Odin are strange and rare. They have many great warriors and fantastical beasts, but we, as the audience, aren't watching these films, even the *Thor* series, from the Asgardian perspective. The movies focus heavily on our world, or at least an approximation of it.

From what we see as watchers of the MCU, the magic of the various heroes and villains is decidedly unnatural.

Stargate SG-1 (Medium Naturalness)

Naturalness is especially interesting when examining it in a technological magic system. By its very nature, most technology was intentionally fabricated by someone. It is unlikely the wilderness of your setting has technology. When was the last time you saw a snail use gunpowder?

But technology is often built using the natural laws and patterns within the setting itself. Returning to the gunpowder example: Gunpowder isn't itself natural, but its materials are. They follow the laws and patterns of chemistry, physics, and thermodynamics. Therefore, gunpowder is unnatural in one sense and natural in another.

The technology in *Stargate SG-1* is no different. All the technology works off of the natural laws of the universe. There isn't anything in the show that remains inexplicable forever. Just as there are no gunpowder-wielding snails in the real world, creatures or objects in the wilds of *Stargate SG-1* don't generate the magical effects produced by technology. But the writers of the show worked hard to make the technology seem reasonable even if it's extremely advanced and often quite alien. That's why the magic of *Stargate SG-1* sits firmly in the middle of the naturalness spectrum.

How to Change It

The easiest way to increase the naturalness of a magic system is to ground it in the setting. Adding creatures or natural phenomena that relate to the core system drives up the naturalness. It doesn't even have to be a direct connection, just simple similarities between what is found in the wild and what is found in the powers of your magic-users.

When it comes to magic systems, and our fiction in general, so much comes down to presentation. If we want the magic to feel more natural and normal, then we can describe the effects in ways that mirror or parallel parts of the setting. We can temper character's reactions to make magic feel like an everyday part of their environment.

If you want to decrease the naturalness instead, simply reverse this process. Sever connections that previously existed. Anything we do to make the magic feel alien, otherworldly, and incomprehensible will decrease its naturalness: twist things about, make a mockery of the setting, or turn the visuals on their heads.

It was tricky getting the naturalness of the Viral Magic System to sit where I wanted. It had to feel more natural than unnatural, but the magical effects within the system were strange and outlandish. One strain solidifies the host's sweat into a bulletproof shell. Another strain transforms blood into a slow but powerful corrosive, disintegrating anything it touches. Still another turned pools of infected blood into teleportation portals.

Maybe it's just me, but none of that feels very natural or in line with the reality I know. Maybe the reality I wish I knew . . . nope. Not even that.

As unnatural as these effects feel, I structured and presented the rest of the system to drive it further up the spectrum. For one, all the effects are tied to natural bodily fluids and functions. Bizarre effects are still firmly tied to something we know. The blood may be corrosive, and sweat may turn into armor, but the blood still carries oxygen, and infected people still sweat when they exert themselves.

Beyond that, the system itself pivots around viruses, what they are, and how they work. Power waxes and wanes along the life cycle of the infection, creating familiar patterns and understandable circumstances.

Altogether, I pulled off a system with medium or medium-high naturalness. But if I wanted to drive that up further, I could.

First, I'd extend the magic further into the setting by having animals use similar abilities. They wouldn't be an exact match, but if the world has otters that can teleport through pools of water, then teleporting through pools of blood doesn't seem quite as far-fetched. And if it were really important to me that the system have high naturalness, I could always tweak the effects into something less outlandish.

To drive the Viral Magic System lower on the naturalness scale, I could make the effects and abilities even weirder (I promise you, I could). Or I could change the core nature of the system. Instead of viruses, everything is caused by biomedical nanites with glitchy programming, or by people growing sick from the malevolent will of an ancient being beyond our understanding. The magical abilities are just a side effect.

So much of this variable is about presentation. Little changes can add up quickly to move a system left or right along this spectrum.

Blueprint Connections

Hard/Soft Axis

We often fear what we don't understand. On top of that, if we don't understand how something fits into the world, it feels unnatural. The level of knowledge available regarding the setting and the magic can influence whether the magic feels like a natural part of the environment. Often times, the hardness and naturalness of a magic system go hand in hand.

Perspective

The perspective you choose while mapping out a magic system impacts its naturalness more than anything else on the Blueprint. A magic system bound by the laws of chemistry will fell more natural to a chemist than to the layman. A big-city politician will likely see the magical creatures of the wilds as less natural than a rancher or forest ranger who works with these creatures every day.

Perspective is *everything* when determining the naturalness of a magic system.

Prevalence

More often than not, high prevalence means high naturalness. Even if it is bizarre and disturbing to us, the fact that it exists around every corner in the story leads to a higher naturalness than otherwise. The opposite is also true. Decrease the prevalence and the magic will feel stranger and less natural.

Ease of Use

What Is It?

Ease of use covers how easy and intuitive it is to effectively and safely utilize the magic. This is yet another sliding scale, ranging from easy to difficult. Some magic systems require years of training, rare materials, and great personal risk to use effectively. Others are wielded with a simple thought.

The Details

Let's start with the most obvious questions: How much training does a magic-user need to perform magic safely? How much does a magic-user need to know or understand about the magic to use it effectively?

One system might be entirely intuitive and instinctual, while another demands training and expertise. How much of a barrier does knowledge, training, and education place before an aspiring magic-user? Maybe the magic-user needs training to prevent any arcane backlash from tearing them apart. If a spell destroys whatever solid matter the user touches, they might need years of practice to ensure it destroys only what they want it to destroy. Time is a resource, and the more time required to successfully train a magic-user, the more difficult the system is to use.

Speaking of time, we also need to consider how long it takes to perform the magic. When it comes to magic, the time it takes to turn a thought or desire into reality has an enormous impact on the usability of the system. Increasing the time doesn't necessarily complicate the magic, but it does make it more difficult to use on the fly, such as in combat and other tense situations.

If the magical effect is passively generated, then no time is required for it to take effect; it simply exists. On the other hand, a two-hour ritual cannot be used reflexively unless the magic-user can hold the magic at the ready until it's needed. Maybe the magic responds instantly to the magic-user's thoughts, but the effect needs time to build and accumulate. All other things being equal, the more time required to effectively perform magic, the harder it is to use the system.

Resource availability or scarcity can complicate a magic system, increasing its difficulty. Having the resources on hand is one thing, but being able to find and acquire them is another. If the only thing a magic-user needs is their internal reserve of energy, then performing magic is no problem. But what if they need the first blossom of spring? Imagine how difficult it would be to find something like that. Or maybe a particular spell requires the teeth of an innocent hanged man. Not only would it be nearly impossible to come by in some settings, these components might also be illegal to obtain or possess.

Anytime special requirements are needed, the magic becomes more difficult to use. What's more, the rarer and more unobtainable the material is, the more difficult the magic becomes.

We've talked about potential time requirements (both in magical training and in casting time) and components that a magic-user might need, but what about the actual actions needed to perform the magic? This can be a spoken word, specific hand gestures, a series of detailed chalk drawings, or a complex ritual. Each additional required action makes the magic more difficult to use.

Let's say a magic-user can reach to the sky, clench their fist, wait thirty seconds as a charge builds, and then rip their hand downward to pull a bolt of lightning from the clouds. Fairly straightforward. Now let's add more complexity. What if the other hand must complete a thirty-second sequence of hand gestures, all executed with precision and timing? That would be much more difficult to manage.

And then there are the elements of focus and intent. If the magic requires absolute focus and a stray thought can disrupt the effect, that's going to make the magic more difficult to use. Maybe the magic does whatever we want it to in theory, but if we aren't clear in our intent, what we *intend* to do and what we *actually get* won't be the same thing. Deliberate intent increases difficulty. Small uncertainties or extra steps for performing an action might compromise the attempt entirely. Each little piece plays a part.

Impact on Your Story

More than anything, the ease of use influences how, where, and when the magic is used. When magic is more difficult to wield, sensible characters are less likely to use it in tense and rapidly evolving situations. In most battles, chase scenes, or other chaotic action sequences, characters don't have time for complex analysis or even a second thought. They resort to instinct and fall back on larger strategy and complex execution only when time allows. If they have a two-day heads-up before they need to use their power, they will have plenty of time to plan and prepare.

The ease of use also impacts how our readers feel about themselves. When characters effectively use difficult systems, your audience feels smart and capable. If they can follow and understand the intricate maneuvers taking place in the story, they will feel as clever and fast on their feet as the characters themselves. When implemented carefully, a magic system's ease of use can affect how the readers feel about themselves and their own abilities, which is a useful tool to understand and develop.

Examples

Mistborn (Medium-Low Ease of Use)

On the surface, Allomancy is fairly easy to use. Magic is performed almost instantly and requires little focus, control, or precision. Although gaining access to some metals to fuel the magic can be tricky, most are easy to come by and cheap to purchase. On top of this, while the system works closely with the laws of physics, a character doesn't actually need to know anything about physics to create magical effects.

All of this points toward a system that's easy to use, but there are still two extremely important factors to consider: skill and experience.

Minimal experience is required to produce the basic effects. In fact, one of the main characters uses Allomancy for years without even realizing what she's doing. While the initial experience barrier is low, the skill cap for this magic system is extremely high. Regardless of the metal or magic effect considered, practice and experience make an enormous difference. The magnitude or reliability of the effects never change, but the effectiveness of the magic-user does.

The difference between a trained and untrained magic-user is like the difference between a nineteen-year-old college student punching you in the leg and a nineteen-year-old soldier striking you in the neck. Technically, the same action is being performed and the power behind it might even be the same, but the results are spectacularly different. In many cases in *Mistborn*, skill and experience often mean the difference between life and death.

This magic system starts out fairly easy to use, but the skill cap is so high that it brings the entire variable up with it. In the end, I see Allomancy as a fairly hard to use magic system. Or more accurately, a system that is fairly hard to use well. Like most variables, there is lots of room for interpretation, but experience is such an important factor that it cannot be ignored.

The Lord of the Rings (Medium-High Ease of Use)

Most of the magic in *The Lord of the Rings* is performed by secondary characters, which means the details are largely unknown to the audience, who mostly experience the novel and film from nonmagical perspectives. Most of what we have are assumptions and Frodo's interactions with the One Ring.

Most magic-users, such as Gandalf, seem able to produce magical effects on demand and at a moment's notice. There are a few scenes that indicate special components might be necessary. The Palantír, for example, is most certainly a required component for any of the scrying that Saruman performs. The wizard's staff seems to be a necessity when performing magic, but it's not entirely clear how essential it really is.

Magical creatures, such as the Ents, seem to have easy access to their magic. No blatant magic is required for the Ents to exist or talk to the trees. It just happens. The same goes for all other magical creatures in the series, unless you count the Nazgûl as creatures. Even then, the use of active magic by magical creatures is rare in the series.

That just leaves the One Ring.

Using the magic of the One Ring, or at least some of the magic, is as simple as putting it on. There's nothing else to do or consider: slip on the ring, turn invisible. It doesn't get much easier to use than that. The main problem with the ring is the inherent danger in using it. Possession of the One Ring slowly warps your mind and soul. And from what we can tell, the more frequently someone uses the ring, the faster this happens. What's more, putting on the ring will draw the attention of the Dark Lord Sauron and his agents.

Combine that together and we're looking at a system that is easy to use but can be quite dangerous.

Marvel Cinematic Universe (High Ease of Use)

Let's look at our heroes.

Apart from his genius intellect, Iron Man's powers are based solely in technology. After Stark created the first suit, anyone with the means could duplicate Iron Man's technology and magical abilities. The suits are also built to function intuitively with the assistance of onboard AI. Anyone can man the suit. It may seem like there is a large barrier, given the education and intelligence needed to design one of these suits, but building or gaining access to a suit is a matter of transference, and using the suit appears to be easy.

The ease of use for Captain America and Thor is even more straightforward. Captain's powers are always present. All he must do is act. His strength, reflexes, and endurance are all a product of the Super Soldier Serum and can be used at a moment's notice. Thor's powers require a little more intentional direction, but if he has access to his powers and his hammer, Mjolnir, he has no issue smashing things, flying, or creating lightning.

Of the original Avengers, the Incredible Hulk has the hardest time using his powers or, more accurately, Bruce Banner has a hard time accessing the Hulk. The Hulk has an easy time accessing its powers. Once Dr. Banner transforms, all of the Hulk's powers are as automatic and easy to access as Captain America's. The problem is that Bruce can't always control when this happens, leading to a lower ease of use.

Once the hero's power is unlocked from the invention of technology, a mystical weapon, or a green rage-monster there are no real complexities of use. Everything seems fairly automatic and intuitive. There are no special time requirements, and only a minimal amount of control, focus, or intent is necessary to create the magical effects.

Every character is different in their own way. The logic and patterns of one hero's magic cannot reliably be applied to all the others. That means we have to average everything together as best we can. With that in mind, the magic of the MCU sits near the easy end of the spectrum.

Stargate SG-1 (Medium Ease of Use)

Some of the technological devices of *Stargate SG-1* are easy to use (the Ma'Tok staff, a Goa'uld weapon), and some are unwieldy and difficult to manage properly and safely (the healing sarcophagus). All the technology requires at least some special knowledge, training, or materials. Some devices require more skill than others to wield safely. Overall, this leads to a system with perfectly average ease of use.

How to Change It

To tweak ease of use, we modify the time involved, the complexity of knowledge, necessary actions, required components, and so on.

I designed the Viral Magic System to fall on the more difficult side of the spectrum. All the magical effects occur passively on their own, meaning there is no need for focus and intention. In that sense, the magic is automatic and thus easy to use, but I made it more difficult in other ways.

For one, time is a large factor in the Viral Magic System. A magic-user has to wait for the sickness to reach its peak before the magic is at its most powerful. And even then, some strains require even more time for the effect they produce to run its course. For example, when infected with one strain, a magic-user's blood can disintegrate any inorganic matter, but this breakdown process takes time, even when the virus is at its peak of power.

I also used the infected blood of the magic-user as a necessary component for specific magic strains. In the one above, the infected has to spread their blood over a surface for the breakdown to occur. In the Portal Strain, which allowed teleportation between pools of blood, the magic-user has to make blood pools large enough for objects or people to pass through. A simple enough concept, but incredibly dangerous when you consider the quantities of blood we're talking about.

Experience and cleverness also factor into ease of use. No experience or education is needed to access the magic (transference). Simple exposure to the virus is enough for that. But once a user has the magic, experience and critical thinking turn an odd magical phenomenon into a useful tool.

What about with other systems? What are some ways we could modify them?

Toy with time. Maybe add a lengthy ritual that only unlocks the magical abilities for a short time. A ritual grants a magic-user flight, but the ability lasts for only twenty seconds. Perhaps magical potions can be prepared in advance, but they have a long production time or a short shelf life. After performing a mind-control spell, maybe it takes several days for the target to succumb.

If we add components to the equation, it's even easier to increase or decrease the difficulty. Perhaps the magic-users need freshly dug soil in order to create a defensive wall. Simple enough, but what if the quality of the soil matters? To build the strongest wall, the magic-user might need earth with high iron and clay content. Do they have soil with that combination nearby? What if it's difficult to get? Maybe the soil doesn't work at all unless mixed with bonemeal ground during a full moon. With every requirement we add, the magic becomes more difficult to use effectively.

Of course, there's always safety to consider. Maybe the magic is easy to use, but whatever the magic-user does to another person, they also do to themselves. If they light an enemy on fire, the magic-user bursts into flames as well. If they heal an ally, the magic-user's own wounds begin to close. Perhaps the magic is extremely violent, such as generating an explosion, and the magic-user can't cast the spell far enough away to escape the impact.

And what about control and intent? The spell could be so delicate and the required concentration so intense that a fly landing on the magic-user's nose could disrupt everything, with catastrophic results. Perhaps healing works only when you truly want to heal someone. If there are any lingering or buried feelings of ill will or frustration, the magic could make the wound even worse. Maybe the magic-user goes to light a candle and ends up setting the entire room ablaze because their intent wasn't clear enough.

There are so many options, I could write a book just about ease of use . . . and maybe I will.

Blueprint Connections

Hard/Soft Axis

All other things being equal, the more someone knows or understands about the magic, the easier it will be to use. This isn't a direct correlation, but a harder system will have less guesswork involved.

Rational/Irrational Axis

Rational systems tend to be easier to use because the magic-user can use logic and understanding to find new applications for the system. Irrational systems aren't more difficult to use, just less intuitive.

Source

Magic systems with internal sources of power are easier to use than those with external sources of power. It's a simple matter of access. If the magic is always present, that's one less thing for the user to think about and manage. It's simply there.

And, all other things being equal, renewable or finite magic sources make using magic more complicated. Now, in addition to simply performing the magic, the magic-user must monitor and manage their magical reserves lest they run out when they need them most. Efficiency of effort and planning on how to renew a power reserve become important considerations, further complicating the process and dividing the magic-user's attention.

Prevalence

This is a one-way connection. An easier magic system to use is one more people will use, and when more people use it, there's a greater chance of it appearing in the story and with greater frequency. The prevalence itself, however, does not directly impact the system's ease of use. A world may be brimming with magical artifacts from a lost civilization, but that doesn't guarantee they will be easy to use.

Reliability

Unreliable magic is not easy to use. That doesn't mean a reliable system is always an easy system, but if you don't know what the magic is going to do when you tap into it, it's difficult to use it effectively. Every time a magic-user generates a magical effect, they are taking a gamble. Even if they have ways to influence the outcome, any degree of randomness and inconsistency ultimately reduces ease of use.

Transference

Transference and ease of use sometimes seem connected, or even the same thing, but they are not connected. Transference determines whether a person has access to the magic at all. Ease of use is all about how easy it is to use the magic once accessed. But education connects these roles. If training is required to perform magic of any kind, then it affects transference. If education simply makes a magic-user more skilled or more effective, or grants them a wider range of abilities, then it affects ease of use.

Reliability

What Is It?

Reliability is the extent to which the magic reproduces the expected results. As with many of the other variables, this is a sliding scale from high reliability to low reliability. In a high-reliability system, a magic-user can trust the magic to perform the way they need it to when they need it to. If a system has low reliability, the magic-user takes a gamble that the magic will produce the result they want.

The Details

To clear this up a bit, let's return to the simple magic system we discussed in the chapters on the types of magic. In the system, the user has a red button and a blue button, each of which generates a single magical effect. When they press the red button, flames erupt from the ground before them. When they press the blue button, shards of ice erupt outward around the magic-user.

The hard/soft axis indicates how much we know. After pressing both buttons, the magic-user potentially knows the entire system. The rational/irrational axis indicates whether logic can be applied to the results. The effects seem to be color coded: the fire behaves like fire, and the ice behaves like ice. We know what the buttons do and how the effects behave, but does the same thing happen every time we push the buttons?

If the same thing happens every time a magic-user tries to generate a specific effect, and in the exact same way, the system has high reliability. If there is a change in the nature of the results or the behavior of the effect, or if there's a chance for the magic to fail altogether, the system has low reliability.

This can mean any number of things. For one, the magic might not work all the time. A magic-user may try to produce an effect and nothing happens. It might be a gamble and works only a percentage of the time. Something could disrupt or disperse the magic, or even break the magic entirely.

And it may not just be the magic itself that causes this unreliability. This is another place where limitations, specifically countermeasures, can come into play. If the desired magic effect is produced every single time, no matter the environment or what anyone does or says, we can rely on the magic. If someone can do or say something that interrupts our magic, then the reliability begins to drop.

On the other hand, the magic may reliably produce an effect, but the nature of the result varies. Something always happens when we press the blue button, but the result isn't always the same. Someone presses the button once and a burst of ice shards erupts around them. They press the button again and this time snow falls. When they press the button a third time, the magic-user is entombed in a protective casing of ice. We know we will get something magical when we push the blue button, but we don't know exactly what it will be. This drives the reliability of the button magic lower on the reliability spectrum.

When building our magic systems, we also need to explore the reliability of any patterns and rules we've established. We could build any number of patterns or correlations into the system to make it more rational, but are those rules ever broken? How many exceptions exist within the system? Broken rules and exceptions lower reliability.

Impact on Your Story

The reliability of our magic system will have a large impact on whether magic-users and readers trust it. Reliability in a magic system equals control. Systems with high reliability tend to feel more utilitarian and scientific. Less reliable magic systems often feel volatile, mysterious, and dangerous. On top of that, a reliable magic system can also provide a sense of internal cohesion within the system and world. This helps the characters and the audience feel like they understand more than they actually do.

Overall, the ability to plan and trust in the magic will have much greater effect on the characters and plot. If the magic system is extremely reliable, the users know the magic will work when they need it to. Their entire plan for dealing with a conflict may pivot around the magic without fear of it failing. That said, if something does go wrong, it could throw their entire plan into chaos.

Also, magic-users are more likely to experiment, learn, and train with reliable magic systems than an unreliable one. If the magic is unreliable, that limits a magic-user's ability to train or plan with it. If a certain effect works only 10 percent of the time, the magic-user probably won't rely on it as their main path to success. That would be foolish. They can plan in case it does work, but smart characters will have backups.

If used properly, unreliable magic can build a great deal of tension in a scene or story. The characters may have tried every option, and the only choice remaining is to try using the magic. But they don't trust it. They don't know if it will perform the way they need, and there could be catastrophic consequences depending on what happens. That kind of gamble is easiest to build with a low-reliability magic system.

Let's shift over to our example systems to see how it all plays out for them.

Examples

Mistborn (High Reliability)

If a character can perform Allomancy, then they always have that ability. If an Allomancer has the appropriate metal available and tries to burn it, they will produce the magical effect 100 percent of the time. At no point in any of the first three books does a magic user try to burn metal and find that they cannot. There are cases where the effect produced isn't noticeable or the user doesn't have the necessary fuel, but the magic is still performing exactly as it should.

This leaves Allomancy with an incredibly high level of reliability.

The Lord of the Rings (High Reliability)

The magic in *The Lord of the Rings* is just as tricky to pin down as ever. We are seldom in the heads of the characters performing the magic. It's possible that, at some point, Gandalf, Sauron, or Saruman tried and failed to use their magic, but we never know. The only point-of-view character shown using magic is Frodo when he slips on the One Ring.

With that being the only data available, *The Lord of the Rings* seems to have a magic system every bit as reliable as Allomancy. If Frodo puts on the One Ring, he will turn invisible. This happens without fail every time he, or anyone else, does this. That's all there is to it. Another system with high reliability.

Marvel Cinematic Universe (Medium-High Reliability)

Whenever a hero or villain in the Marvel Cinematic Universe attempts to use their powers, they are usually successful. They all know what they can do, and can trust in their abilities to perform when they need them to.

Captain America, for example, will always have his increased strength, endurance, resilience, and enhanced healing capabilities. As long as Thor has access to Mjolnir, and is deemed worthy to wield it, his powers are always at his command when he tries to use them. For these characters, it is never a question whether the magic will work, but a question of whether they can use it well enough to resolve the situation at hand.

This does vary slightly between magic-users, however, and there are a few instances where a hero's abilities fail to activate, or do something unexpected. Iron Man's suit, for example, is durable and fairly reliable, but it can break, fail, or perform in an unexpected fashion.

And then there's the Incredible Hulk.

On the one hand, the actual traits and abilities are as reliable as Captain America's, but Banner's ability to change into the Hulk is not. Sometimes the Hulk does what he's asked, but not always. At times, the Hulk takes over against Banner's will, and in other situations he refuses to appear at all, despite Banner's insistence.

Exceptions do exist, but the magic system overall sits in the medium-high range of the reliability spectrum.

Stargate SG-1 (Medium-High Reliability)

The technology of the *Stargate* universe is an especially interesting example of a reliable magic system. For the most part, any technological magic system is going to have higher reliability than a more traditional magic system. After all, what's the point of a device that works only a fraction of the time? But in this series, the writers manage an interesting balance of reliability across the different forms of technology.

Each individual piece of technology reproduces its magical effects reliably, regardless of its origins. But can characters rely on this technology to perform in the first place? Not always.

Much of the technology is just as reliable as you might expect. Guns, ship engines, and the Stargates themselves work most of the time. But most of the time is not the same as always. There are numerous instances throughout the series where these technologies fail or perform strangely. When this does happen, it usually becomes an obstacle for that episode or season.

That said, there are other parts of the system that are less reliable than the occasional accident or breakdown can account for.

Over the course of the series, the characters find many devices were created by the Ancients, one of the most advanced races known to have existed, including the Stargates. Technology created by the Ancients is less reliable than the other technology in *Stargate SG-1*. If a piece of Ancient tech is fully functional when the characters find it, however, it often remains reliable, but that rarely happens. The characters frequently discover devices that are broken or breaking, and since they have no good way of repairing technology from the Ancients, the reliability of those devices, and the magic system as a whole, drops.

Moreover, characters uncover even rarer forms of even more powerful technology with even lower reliability. When the characters do gain access to this technology, they can't always make it work. In fact, getting the device in question working before something terrible happens is often a major plot point. If the devices were more reliable, the characters could switch them on and use them without a problem.

All things considered, this leaves the magic in *Stargate SG-1* on the medium-high end of the spectrum.

How to Change It

In order to change the reliability of a magic system, we as creators need to alter two things: replication and trustworthiness.

As of the writing of this book, the Viral Magic System sits somewhere around the medium-high end of the reliability spectrum. On one hand, the magic is always active. As long as the virus is present in the host, the magical effects exist. On top of that, the magic always performs the same. The thing is, while the presence and nature of the effects are reliable, their magnitude isn't.

The potency of the magic effects is entirely dependent on the number of virions within the host's body. This number will increase or decrease from day to day according to the state of the illness within the host. And just because the magic has a certain level of strength the first time you contract the disease, that doesn't mean it will be as strong the second time. It will vary from person to person depending on their health and numerous other conditions.

But what if we wanted to change that?

To increase the reliability, we can add phases and durations to the illness. It's easier for a magic-user to plan how and when to use the magic if they know it will be strongest on the second and third day of the illness. That would be the best way to increase reliability without compromising the core theme of the system.

And how would we decrease reliability in the Viral Magic System? In the original system, I have each magical effect assigned to a specific viral strain. We could remove that structure entirely and randomize the magical effect every time someone contracts a virus. The nature of the effect might even change as the illness waxes and wanes.

If we wanted to take it a step further, what if specific environments suppressed the magical effects of the virus? If heat and humidity factor into the performance of the magic, magic-users can't trust their abilities in specific situations.

One of the simplest ways to build reliability is to show more of the magic. The more information we provide, the more the characters and readers will trust it. If they see something only once or twice, they won't know whether it will behave that way every time. But if they see the same thing ten times, they will trust it more.

To take things the other direction, we simply need to break the pattern and defy expectations. Imagine if the magic behaved the same the first twenty times it was used, but then did something different on the twenty-first attempt. That would likely shake a magic-user's trust of the system. Even if the magic is highly reliable, even one exception will make a big difference. This change could be anything. We could add a new effect: instead of producing a glowing orb of light, a spell or magic-user produces a globe of acid.

Another option would be to break an established rule or limitation. If, for example, the magic system adheres to the conservation of mass, introducing even a single magical effect that creates matter from nothing would lower the system's overall reliability. We could even go so far as to show the magic breaking down altogether. Something went wrong, and now it won't work until it has been repaired. This is frequently used with technological magic systems, but the principle is applicable everywhere.

If magic requires a wand as a focus, what happens when too much power is channeled through it? What if someone cracks it or steps on it? Does it break? Can the magic-user perform rudimentary magic without it, or are their abilities effectively broken as well?

All these questions, and their answers, will affect the perceived reliability of the magic system.

Rather than showing more of the system, we could also show less. By hiding patterns, rules, and other system elements, we can make the magic appear random and less reliable than it really is. For example, the position of a magic-user's left hand might change a magical effect generated by their right. When the left hand is by the hip, the right hand generates a field of zero gravity. But when the magic-user raises the left hand to shoulder height, the right hand creates a repelling force field.

As the creators of the system, we know what the influencing elements are, but the characters and readers might not. To them, the system will seem unreliable until the connection is made.

We could even make the results of the magic truly random by creating a table of effects and determining success and failure rates. Then, when a character wants to use the magic in the story, we can roll dice or use a random number generator to see what happens. This kind of unreliability is most common in games, but this could be an interesting way for us as authors to throw unexpected twists and complications into an otherwise simple plot.

Blueprint Connections

Hard/Soft Axis

The hard/soft spectrum is all about knowledge and understanding of the magic, and the level of knowledge available to a magic-user plays a big part in whether a system seems reliable. If the magic-user knows only part of how the system works, or if their understanding doesn't match reality, then the system may seem unreliable when it's actually reliable.

Rational/Irrational Axis

There is a connection between the rationality and reliability of your magic system, but they are not the same. Rational magic systems are predictable, and the more rational and predictable they are, to magic-users and readers, the easier it is to apply and implement the magic within that system in useful ways.

Ease of Use

If the magic doesn't perform reliably, then it can't be trusted to perform as desired in a time of need. If the magic can't be trusted, then using it becomes more of a gamble, and the system becomes more difficult to use effectively.

Consistency

What Is It?

Consistency appears last on the Blueprint for a reason. Consistency looks at if and how much all the other variables in the system deviate from their designated setting. It also considers the thematic and tonal consistency across all effects and magic-users within the magic system. If there are a lot of exceptions and outliers in the system, this is how to quantify them.

The Details

When examining the consistency of a magic system, we want to compare all the evidence of the magic we can. The perspective chosen determines whether the available evidence is an accurate depiction of the whole. But as the creators, we need to consider the system in its entirety, which means examining every magic-user, magical creature, and magical effect side by side.

But what are we looking for?

We want to know how much the abilities, effects, tone, and other aspects change from one sample to another. So far we've established seven other variables for our system. Are those settings absolute, or is there some wiggle room?

In addition to accounting for the other variables, we also need to consider the consistency of effects. Does every magic-user, creature, and phenomenon produce the same magical effects, or do they vary from instance to instance? Maybe a giant scorpion uses magic to move and mold stone and earth around it. If humanity performs the same effects in the exact same way, the system is consistent. Maybe human magic-users can shape stone, but the rules and limitations are different from those faced by the scorpion. In that case, the consistency is lower. And if every single magic-user has a different magical ability, then the consistency is extremely low.

But it's more than just the technical result at play here. We also want to look at how the effect manifests. If every magic-user shapes stone by touching and molding it like clay, there is thematic consistency between them. But what if one user molds it like clay and another forms spectral tools to cut and join the stone? Variation in the style and execution of the effect lowers the consistency of the system.

Examples

Mistborn (High Consistency)

Magic systems don't get much more consistent than Allomancy from the *Mistborn* series.

Every single magic-user performs the same magical effects in exactly the same way. This is true for most of the variables as well. With a few exceptions, transference is the same across the board: you're either born an Allomancer or you're not. The source is the same for everyone, and it is just as reliable to nobles and street rats alike. Even the strength of the effect is consistent. It doesn't matter how tired a magic-user has become or how low they are on metal, the power output will be the same.

And what about cohesion among the powers? The powers exist in pairs that intuitively couple with or counter each other. Burning steel pushes metal away from the user while burning iron pulls metal toward the user. Bronze allows the user to sense others using magic nearby, while copper hides nearby use of magic.

Brandon Sanderson uses metals and alloys to link all the Mistborn powers together thematically. Even though there's no actual connection between the types of metals and the powers they produce, the repeated use of metals creates strong thematic cohesion within the system.

All of this combines to create a magic system with high levels of consistency throughout.

The Lord of the Rings (Low Consistency)

The magic from *The Lord of the Rings* is such a mash-up that its level of consistency is difficult to pin down. The effects we see are widely varied and contain no apparent connection. The only thing connecting them is the fact that it's all magic. The effects themselves vary; even how the magic looks and sounds is inconsistent between magic-users.

Marvel Cinematic Universe (Low Consistency)

The magic of the Marvel Cinematic Universe has been interesting to study and map. Each hero and villain works differently. Nowhere is this more evident than in the thematic and tonal elements of each superhero. Each has their own theme and motif, and with the exception of a few core abilities, there is no real cohesion between the powers and the magic-users themselves. We do see animal themes crop up Black Panther, Ant-Man, Spider-Man, Black Widow, Hawkeye but what they are and the powers that come with them often have little connection.

Because of this, the magic in the MCU has fairly low levels of consistency.

Stargate SG-1 (Medium Consistency)

The technology in *Stargate SG-1* is consistent in some areas and inconsistent in others.

If we look at the effects available to the magic-users, the system is consistent. Every character can access and use most of, if not all, the devices discovered in the show. They have to gain access and learn how first (transference and ease of use), but the effects are available.

Some of the other system variables are a bit more flexible. Prevalence and reliability, for example, fluctuate depending on the technology. Some gadgets and effects are commonplace and others are rare treasures. Certain devices are robust and hardy in their design and never seem to fail. Others are much more temperamental.

Finally, when looking at technological magic systems, it can be difficult to determine a sense of cohesion. In many stories, the only theme is that the magic functions like machines do, off the same principles in our reality. *Stargate SG-1* took this a bit further and developed a variety of stylistic motifs to go with the technology. The Goa'uld design and architecture, for example, heavily embraces ancient Egyptian mythology. It's not just the Goa'uld who do this. The devices of each race have their own look and feel, even if the end results were all the same.

Combine all of this together and you have a system with a moderate level of consistency.

Blueprint Connections

Consistency is a unique piece of the Blueprint. It doesn't influence the place-ment of the other variables as much as it acts as a reference for how much we deviate from said placement. We might mark one magic system as having medium-low transference, but if that system also has low consistency, that transference rating has a greater likelihood of fluctuating.

On top of this, consistency might affect some variables more than others. In systems with low consistency in certain variables, keep your original indicators for the affected variables, but also highlight the regions where the outliers exist.

Notes

THE LAST section of the Blueprint is for notes. Any ideas, concepts, or connections that don't fit anywhere else should go here.

While this section can contain absolutely anything, there are a few stray concepts worth exploring. None of these things impact the core system itself, but they can be incredibly useful when it comes time to write the magic into a story.

Common Descriptions and Effects

Everyone has their favorite colors, tools, techniques, and words. The way people view and describe the world around them can be incredibly personal. Certain words and ways of speaking serve as verbal fingerprints for specific characters. We can use this to our advantage.

Take the perspective at hand and consider how this might apply to the magic system. What effects would that perspective favor over others? What descriptive words would that perspective use when referencing the magic or magic-users? Is the magic, to that perspective, an abomination and an affront to nature, or is it a precious gift to be learned and used? Do particular magic-users prefer wielding one element of the magic over others, such as wielding ice? Or maybe they prefer mind-bending illusions?

History

How have the characters interacted with the magic in the past? What important magical events have occurred? When did the magic first arrive? How long has it been around? Have the main characters used it before? How often?

The list of questions goes on and on. While this has nothing to do with the magic itself, it never hurts to have these notes. Taking a few minutes to jot down notes like this can help tremendously when writing or outlining a story. New connections, options, and potential character conflicts will all rise to the surface.

And that's the entire Blueprint.

Example Worksheets

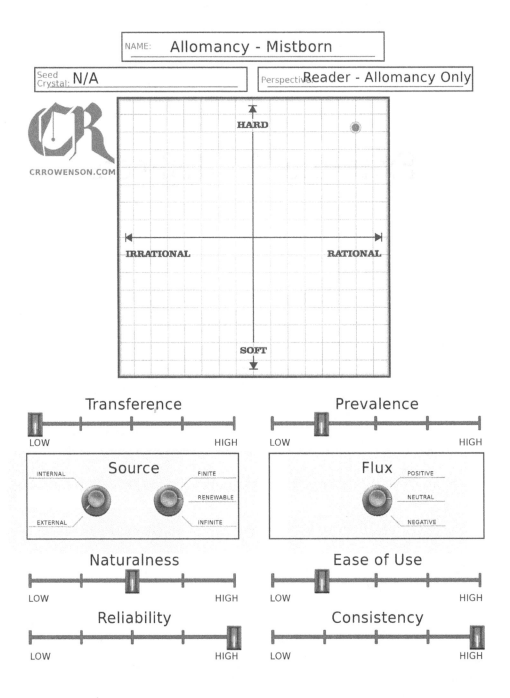

NAME: Allomancy - Mistborn

Seed Crystal: N/A

Perspective: Reader - Allomancy Only

HARD

IRRATIONAL   RATIONAL

SOFT

Transference — LOW / HIGH

Prevalence — LOW / HIGH

Source — INTERNAL / EXTERNAL / FINITE / RENEWABLE / INFINITE

Flux — POSITIVE / NEUTRAL / NEGATIVE

Naturalness — LOW / HIGH

Ease of Use — LOW / HIGH

Reliability — LOW / HIGH

Consistency — LOW / HIGH

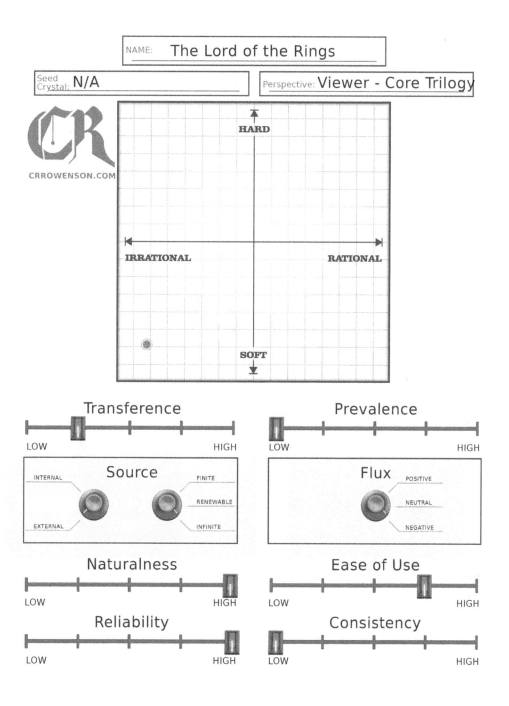

NAME: The Lord of the Rings

Seed Crystal: N/A

Perspective: Viewer - Core Trilogy

HARD

IRRATIONAL   RATIONAL

SOFT

Transference
LOW   HIGH

Prevalence
LOW   HIGH

Source
INTERNAL   FINITE
                RENEWABLE
EXTERNAL   INFINITE

Flux
POSITIVE
NEUTRAL
NEGATIVE

Naturalness
LOW   HIGH

Ease of Use
LOW   HIGH

Reliability
LOW   HIGH

Consistency
LOW   HIGH

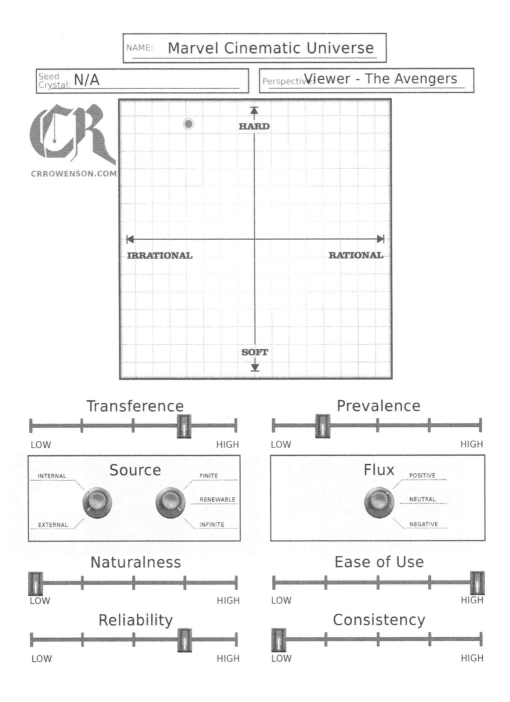

NAME: Marvel Cinematic Universe

Seed Crystal: N/A

Perspective: Viewer - The Avengers

HARD

IRRATIONAL   RATIONAL

SOFT

CRROWENSON.COM

Transference
LOW   HIGH

Prevalence
LOW   HIGH

Source
INTERNAL   FINITE
                  RENEWABLE
EXTERNAL   INFINITE

Flux
POSITIVE
NEUTRAL
NEGATIVE

Naturalness
LOW   HIGH

Ease of Use
LOW   HIGH

Reliability
LOW   HIGH

Consistency
LOW   HIGH

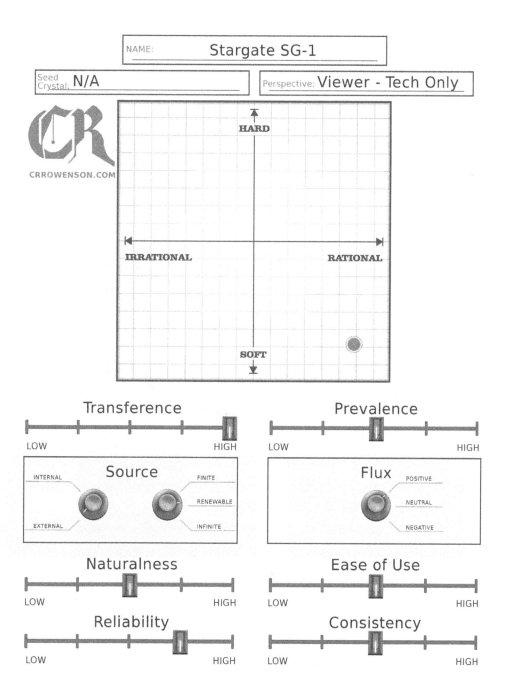

NAME: Stargate SG-1

Seed Crystal: N/A

Perspective: Viewer - Tech Only

HARD

IRRATIONAL — RATIONAL

SOFT

CRROWENSON.COM

Transference
LOW — HIGH

Prevalence
LOW — HIGH

Source
INTERNAL
EXTERNAL
FINITE
RENEWABLE
INFINITE

Flux
POSITIVE
NEUTRAL
NEGATIVE

Naturalness
LOW — HIGH

Ease of Use
LOW — HIGH

Reliability
LOW — HIGH

Consistency
LOW — HIGH

PART FOUR

Working Outside the Blueprint

B Y NOW you should see the power and utility the Blueprint has to offer. In fact, if you've been filling it out as you read, you likely have a better understanding of your magic system than many published authors have of theirs. But as much as I hate to say it, the Blueprint alone won't give you a complete magic system.

In this last portion, we're going to take a quick look at what you can do to fill in any gaps or cracks that might remain in your magic system. This first step is a fairly easy one.

Map Another Blueprint

REMEMBER what we talked about in the chapter on perspective? How you can map more than one Blueprint to a given magic system? In fact, it's extremely beneficial to do so.

Each perspective views and understands your magic system differently, which changes your Blueprint. As you become more comfortable using the Blueprint, you can map out multiple versions of the same system by simply changing the perspective. By covering multiple perspectives, you develop a more comprehensive sense of the magic.

Think of it like this: Any given Blueprint is a single image, a snapshot of the magic system at a specific time and angle. Even the best photographer can't capture a three-dimensional shape with a single photo. They have to move around the object, taking more pictures from new angles and with different lighting. To get a fully defined, three-dimensional understanding of the magic system, we need to do the same.

So pick a new perspective, any perspective, and give it a try. If you're not sure where to start, here are four different perspectives I recommend to everyone.

The Universal Perspective

The universal perspective considers the magic in its entirety and how it fits into the world at large. This is likely the first perspective you adopted with your magic system, but if it wasn't, I highly recommend you do it now.

Calibrate the universal perspective according to the full scope of your story. Does your story stretch across the galaxy, or is it limited to one continent? You can narrow this perspective accordingly.

The Audience Perspective

The way you experience and understand your magic system will be radically different from how your audience experiences or understands it. This isn't a bad thing. You built it from the ground up and know the ins and outs like nobody else ever will, but take a moment to consider your reader. Imagine how you want the magic to appear to them and how you will facilitate that perspective through storytelling.

The Protagonist Perspective

Take what you know about the magic and examine it through your protagonist's eyes. You can get an "in-world glimpse" from any secondary character, but selecting the protagonist perspective can offer you insights into your story and the experience it will deliver. A protagonist is the audience's primary means of experiencing the world and the story. You can use this to your advantage to develop a deeper understanding and control over the audience's journey.

A protagonist that is inexperienced and new to the magic will have good reasons to ask questions, explore, and learn. A more experienced character might share or review the information only when relevant to the immediate situation.

And if all that wasn't enough, you'll simultaneously get a deeper understanding of one of your most important characters. Talk about a win-win scenario.

The Antagonist Perspective

Too many storytellers forget to consider things from the bad guy's point of view. A twisted rival, vengeful outcasts, and dark gods will all experience the magic differently. Exploring these perspectives can provide an excellent counterpoint to your protagonist's perspective. Remember, trying to understand an entire magic system from a single perspective is like trying to capture a three-dimensional object with a single photo.

The antagonist's perspective will allow you to dig into the dark, hidden corners of your magic system. What loopholes have they found? How does the magic shape them, and how do they shape the magic? What do they know, see, or understand that others don't? Exploring your magic system through the antagonist's eyes is a great way to kick-start your plot and find twists and turns you never considered before.

So get into their head and see what that does for you, your magic, and your story. You might be surprised with what you find.

There are countless other perspectives for us to pick up and try, and each one of them has something different to offer. Don't forget, the perspective can be as narrow or as broad as we need it to be. Want to know what the magic looks like to a foreign nation? Map a Blueprint. Considering how a carpenter would use the magic versus how a blacksmith would? Map a Blueprint.

Magic Effects and Abilities

F IRST things first, what are magic effects and abilities? It all comes back to the definition of magic: anything enabling actions beyond our current capability or understanding.

Magic effects and abilities are the specific actions that the magic itself enables. This is what the magic-users actually do when wielding their magic.

Magic effects don't function like the rest of the Blueprint. Magic effects are anything your imagination slaps together, meaning there's no consistent structure or range of effects that apply to every system. In fact, magic effects, as well as limitations and patterns, almost didn't make it onto the Blueprint at all. But you can't have magic without magical effects, so it didn't feel right to leave them out entirely.

This section of the Blueprint is mostly a blank box for you to fill however you see fit. Use it to brainstorm, build mind maps, or even just catalog the effects you know you want in the final system, whatever works best for you.

And don't worry if the list of effects feels generic at first. Once it is set alongside the Blueprint and woven into the story, even the most clichéd magical effect can become new and wondrous again. Just take a look at some of the magical effects from our example systems.

Mistborn

» Fly and leap through the air
» Inflame or soothe another person's emotions
» Sense magic-users in the area
» Prevent others from sensing magic-users
» Enhance all senses simultaneously

» Increase physical attributes (strength, endurance, dexterity)

The Lord of the Rings

» Turn invisible
» Generate light
» Break stone
» Control the minds and actions of others
» Heat metal
» Generate waves of force to lift or throw others

Marvel Cinematic Universe

» Enhanced strength and endurance
» Increased healing and regeneration
» Flying
» Generating and hurling lightning
» Physical transformations
» Focused blasts of energy
» Teleportation

Stargate SG-1

» Faster-than-light space travel
» Flight
» Teleportation
» Invisibility
» Enhanced healing and regeneration
» Genetically encoded technology
» Massive clean power generation

On their own, these magical effects aren't groundbreaking, and they don't need to be. When examined at a high level like this, many magic systems start to look the same and don't stand out until you get into the nitty-gritty.

One hundred different systems can use teleportation and invisibility as magical effects and still feel drastically different. Both *Stargate SG-1* and the MCU have teleportation effects, but one generates them through rippling blue portals and the other through beams of rainbow light. Both *The Lord of the Rings* and the *Mistborn* series have magic to manipulate the minds of others. In *The Lord of the Rings* this effect comes from the corrupting power of the One Ring, and in the *Mistborn* series it comes from amplifying or muting people's emotions.

Remember, creativity lies in combinations, and distinction is in the details. Once you get into the details, your effects, and system as a whole, should begin to feel unique.

Balance

O NCE WE HAVE our Blueprint mapped and our effects listed, it's important to consider the balance of the system. When we talk about balance, we're examining the mechanics of the magic and how they might create power disparities between characters, entities, or organizations.

To be clear, this variable strictly focuses on whether these disparities exist and how easy it is to create them. Don't worry about whether an individual character will abuse the system. That is a narrative decision to be made on a character-by-character and story-by-story basis.

When considering the balance of a magic system, it's best to start with a simple analysis. Does the magic provide an average magic-user an extreme advantage over a person without magic?

It doesn't matter whether the extreme advantage is physical, social, or financial in nature. If an extreme advantage exists, then the system might be unbalanced.

For a more detailed understanding of a system and its inherent balance, let's explore several mechanical variables we can adjust to balance our magic systems.

Frequency

How often can magic-users produce magical effects?

If magic-users can produce magical effects over and over again without end, there is massive potential for a power imbalance. By adding delays and downtime between uses of the magic, you force the magic-user to be more careful and deliberate with their magic. It also provides people without magic a chance to respond, escape, or retaliate.

Duration

Similar to frequency, the longer a magical effect lasts, the more likely it is to unbalance the magic system.

For example, if a magic-user can sap the strength of a target, leaving the target lethargic and slow, this magic effect can have a big impact on an encounter. How much of an advantage does it provide to the magic-user if the effect lasts for a minute? What if it lasts for an hour, or a day? What if it lasts forever? Increasing the duration increases the potential advantage granted to the magic-user.

Let's look at another example.

Temporarily creating an unbreakable shield of energy is a powerful ability, but if it lasts only for a second, the magic-user must use it at just the right time for it to be effective. Imagine what happens if the duration starts lengthening. Now the magic-user has an impenetrable defense lasting minutes, days, or even years.

Magnitude

This piece is fairly straightforward and comes down to a simple question: How powerful is the magical effect?

If a magic-user creates arcane explosions, how powerful are they? Do they have the energy of firecrackers? Grenades? Nuclear warheads? Are the blasts strong enough to break apart stone, or are they just enough to knock over a tower of cards? The magnitude of the effect greatly influences the balance of the magic.

Consider how you might measure the power of a magical effect. It doesn't need to be an exact science, with rigorous measurements. Even simple qualitative measurements (weak, strong, extremely strong) will go a long way toward identifying how easy it is to abuse a magic system.

Area of effect

When a magical effect is produced, how much of an area does it cover? The head of a pin? An entire person? A whole city block?

The larger the area of influence, the less precision is required. If a simple thought can influence dozens of people or destroy an entire building, then there is little chance of the magic-user missing or of the targets evading the effect. There are, of course, situations where being able to focus on an extremely small area is beneficial, but larger effects generally have a greater impact on the balance of a system.

Range

How far can a magic-user send a magical effect? A foot? A mile? A thousand miles? Across solar systems? Or does it require direct contact?

If a magic-user can produce a magical effect anywhere within the radius of several miles, they will be difficult to counter or contend with. Decreasing the effective range decreases the options available to the magic-user. The greater a magic-user's range, the less balanced the system tends to be.

Efficiency

Can a magic-user produce magical effects using less energy or material than others?

If magic allows a character to create a tool or substance ten times faster, or with less material or energy, then there is potential for extreme imbalance, especially in a magic system with a finite or renewable source. In these cases, a more efficient magic-user can produce more magic than the average magic-user while expending the same amount of energy. An efficient magic-user can also run on fumes, so to speak, when the average magic-user can't.

Malleability

So far, you've considered the frequency at which the magic can be performed, the duration of the effects, the magnitude of the effects, the area of effect, the range, and the level of efficiency. Now let's examine how rigid those variables are and how much control the magic-user has over them. More flexibility means more options, and more options means a greater potential for imbalance.

Consider a magic-user that can put people and creatures within 100 feet of them to sleep. That is a powerful ability, but it comes with drawbacks. What if the magic-user doesn't want to put everyone around them to sleep, like, say, their allies? If there is no flexibility in the magic, this becomes a risky solution, but it's more balanced than if they had the freedom to change the area of effect. If concentration can bring the area of effect down to within five feet of the magic-user, or if the magic-user can shape the magic so it wouldn't affect certain people, these options increase control and power, further unbalancing the magic system.

Success Rate

What are the chances the magical effect will lead to the outcome the magic-user intended?

Consider the following example: A magic-user creates a ball of supercooled water and sends it flying toward a target, hoping it will instantly freeze around them and lock them in place. What are the chances that everything will play out how the magic-user hoped? Can the target dodge the incoming water, or does it materialize around them without a chance to evade? Can the target block the attack with a special object? Can they counter it with other magic? Is there any way the magic-user's target can prevent the desired outcome from occurring?

Impact of Balance on Your Story

With an unbalanced system, you run a real risk of having overpowered characters, and overpowered characters can damage your story. Sometimes they make great villains, but for the most part they rob the story of suspense and make it difficult for readers to suspend their disbelief. If the protagonist has unlimited power, then no obstacles can stop them. If there are no obstacles between the protagonist and their goals, then there's no conflict. If there's no conflict, then there's no story.

That's why, when abuse of magic does exist, the antagonists are often the ones with the power advantage.

Something else to consider is that imbalances can work themselves out over time: a coup against the abusers, the development of better countermeasures against the abuser, the emergence of new magic-users, or even some kind of industrial or societal revolution.

This isn't to say that an unbalanced magic system is a bad magic system. It just needs to be managed differently. If a magic system is unbalanced, the world, the characters, and the story itself can feel it, and will react to it. Balanced magic systems fade into the background more easily. Creators can sprinkle them over everything without upsetting the balance. Unbalanced systems offer more plot hooks, so you can always start there if your well of story ideas is running dry.

Either way, consider how you want the magic to factor into the world and story when exploring whether a system is balanced.

Magic-System Limitations

A MAGIC-SYSTEM limitation is anything you put in place to regulate the use or scope of your magic system.

The need for magical effects and abilities is fairly obvious. Without these actions or abilities, there is no magic at all. But why do we need limitations? Won't they force us into a corner and limit our creativity?

Not quite.

Good limitations will make the system unique and interesting both for the characters and the audience. They will even help us as creators. We are at our most creative when we have restrictions and problems to work around. Limitations can be our best friends.

On top of that, if we implement a magic system with zero limitations, then the story will have zero conflict.

We, as audience members, don't want easy solutions in our stories. We want to experience struggle, strife, and effort through the protagonist. That way, if they achieve victory, it feels earned and satisfying. With no restrictions on what they can do, a protagonist will be boring and overpowered, and the antagonist will be unbeatable. Neither makes for an enjoyable story.

And if that wasn't enough, limitations simply make magic systems more interesting. In "Sanderson's Second Law," Brandon Sanderson talks about exactly that. He discusses how Superman's weaknesses, not his strengths, are what make him interesting. Why is he weak to Kryptonite? How do bad guys continue to find fragments of it to use against Superman? How can he resolve a situation without compromising his code of ethics? These are all fascinating questions that can lead to phenomenal story arcs, hooks, and twists.

Suffice it to say, limitations are an important part of any magic system. In fact, they're so important that I wrote a workbook designed to help magic-builders in this exact way called *Restrictions May Apply: Building Limitations for Your Magic*. If you want a deeper dive into the topic and exercises to help you along the way, give it a look.

This section of the Deluxe Blueprint is designed to function just like the area for magical effects and abilities. It's a blank canvas for exploring and identifying the limitations of your magic system.

A great place to start building limitations is by cutting back on the number of magic effects or abilities. Restricting the overall capabilities of an individual magic-user may be all the magic system needs.

If it's not enough, consider the three *C*'s of magic system limitations: costs, consequences, and countermeasures.

Costs are, quite simply, something a magic-user must pay, provide, or expend in order to perform the magic: money for expensive components, the consumption of rare material, or the sacrifice of memories. Whatever it is, something is lost in exchange for the generation of a magical effect. Costs can be minuscule and insignificant or massive and overwhelming. Builder's choice.

Consequences are anything that results from using the magic. It can be a direct result, such as the user burning themselves with the fire magic, or it can be indirect, like a user being banished for the practice of necromancy. The manner, immediacy, and scope of the consequences are entirely up to the builder. In general, the more severe the consequence, the greater a limitation it places on the magic-users.

Countermeasures are any means, magical or mundane, that can counteract or cancel magic. Warding circles, antimagic charms, and Kryptonite are all examples of magical countermeasures. These make for interesting limitations because they are employed against the magic-users rather than something the magic-user pays or suffers to cast the magic. Countermeasures are a tremendous way to level the playing field between magic-users and people without magic.

To understand limitations, let's consider them in a magic system where the magic-users can sing to generate magical effects, but afterward the magic-users can never again speak without generating some kind of magical effect. Additionally, loud noises or disruptions in the air can warp and distort the magical songs and break the magical effects.

In this case, the cost is the magic-user's voice, as they can no longer speak normally. If they try to speak without song, the generation of uncontrollable magic effects serves as an unpredictable consequence to their actions. This is a huge sacrifice that could balance other aspects of the system. You could also add a time limit to the restriction so the magic-users can freely use their voice again after a certain refractory period.

And finally, other people could use noise-canceling speaker systems or large fans to disrupt the sound waves or drown out the singing. This offers nonmagical characters a plethora of options to use as countermeasures against the singing magic-users.

If you're still struggling to understand or come up with limitations, I highly recommend picking up a copy of *Restrictions May Apply*.

Perception

O NE OF THE MOre amorphous features of any magic system, perception considers how someone from a given perspective feels about and experiences the magic. A person's perception of the magic includes their personal feelings, opinions, and beliefs about the magic system as well as the sensations they experience from it. This is closely tied to perspective, but since it doesn't directly impact any other variables on the Blueprint, it has been broken out into this section of the book.

This is where you can explore how the magic manifests, its connections to the characters, what the characters experience, cultural preferences and taboos, whether it's seen as good or evil, and much more.

The experience of performing magic and how it manifests, while mostly flavor, greatly impacts how it will be perceived by characters and even your audience. Magic that is beautiful and pleasant to perform might be sought after or even seen as holy, while painful and disturbing magic will likely be viewed differently. I mean, would you rather see magic that causes flowers to bloom or magic that opens your mind to living nightmares with every use?

Which brings up the concept of good and evil. You don't need to decide whether the system itself is inherently good or evil. You may decide it is a force of corruption and is evil to the core, or it might just be a powerful tool and the good or evil comes from how you use it. Regardless, it is important to determine how it's viewed by the people in your story. Every magic-user, culture, nation, or collection of people will have different opinions about the magic in your system. Personal history with the magic, how it defies or connects to personal beliefs and values, and access to the magic all factor into people's perception of the magic.

On a similar note, be sure to consider whether the magic is a desirable thing to have. Good or evil, it might be a powerful blessing that many are willing to sacrifice for, or it could come at a terrible price even though it is for the good of mankind. There's no limit to the different ways this can all play out.

Finally, make sure to explore the status of the magic-users among those without magic. Are they revered, hated, or somewhere in between? How do people feel about a magic-user that has gained new powers? What if they have lost their powers, or were supposed to have them but never did?

Take time to think through the different relationships that can exist between the magic, magic-users, and people without magic, as well as how someone from your chosen perspective will interpret them.

Perception offers an enormous amount of potential for plot and conflict, making it a terrific tool for story development. Bitter rivals might fight to the death over a revered and desirable item. Cults might hunt an innocent character simply for possessing magic. Your protagonist might focus on keeping aspects of the magic hidden from the rest of the population. The list goes on and on. The perspective you build up for the magic can determine what kinds of conflicts are available and how they play out.

Don't worry about writing yourself into a corner. For every opinion that exists, there will be those that counter it. You can easily have plots casting the same magic system in both a positive and negative light. It's all about how you craft the perspective, perception, and story.

Miscellaneous Actions

Identify Themes, Patterns, and Equations

Some authors prefer a more disjointed and random magic system, and that's perfectly fine. No one type or style of magic system is better than the others. But taking the time and energy to generate some of these connections can make a magic system feel cohesive, orderly, and unique.

Fortunately, humans are pattern-seeking creatures, so much so that we often find patterns and correlations that aren't actually there. This is something we can use to our advantage when building magic systems, even ones that are totally random.

What forces, ratios, or principles apply to the magic? Does magic ignore gravity? What about conservation of energy? Does every spell unleashed in the world truly come back on the caster threefold? Does the system have a particular motif, material, or subject matter? What subjects could you study to form a more cohesive magic system? Are there things that make different magic-users similar to one another, even if the effects they produce are radically different?

This step isn't always necessary, but it can be a ton of fun and an easy way to quickly make your magic system into something distinct.

Align It with Your Story.

I don't always have a story in mind when I start a magic system; the magic itself is often enough to keep me going. Unless you're a little strange like me and build magic systems for the sake of building them, odds are good you want to add the magic system into a story. Now we need to make sure they complement each other instead of weakening each other.

Checking the alignment of your magic and story is all about finding those ways they connect and resonate. If you want to tell a sweet romance story set in a secondary-world fantasy setting, you need to take that into consideration when building the magic system. A magic system centered around the power of emotional bonds and consent would resonate with a sweet romance story better than a system focused on harvesting the organs of magical creatures. See what I mean? Both can be made to work, but one is better aligned with the core of the story.

So how are your magic system and story connected? Take a look at the character concepts, theme, plot, setting, and genre you're shooting for and see how they line up or contrast with the magic system. Maybe the consequences of using magic mirror the theme of dealing with addition. The magic might have quirks or limitations that force the characters to grow and change to develop their powers. You might even structure your plot so elements of the magic system are pivotal elements of the key plot points.

This isn't to say the magic needs to be perfectly aligned with every element of your story. Contrast and dissonance can be powerful storytelling tools as long as you are deliberate in their use.

Do you want to know the best part? At least, I think it's the best part. You don't have to change the Blueprint to improve the alignment of your system. It may come down entirely to what you show and how you show it. That means a single magic system can be applied to and aligned with a wide variety of stories without changing a single variable on the Blueprint.

So take some time and check the alignment of your story and magic system. Explore the ways they tie together and generally enhance each other.

Break, Inspect, and Repair

This is your chance to make sure your magic system doesn't have any inconsistencies, loopholes, or power exploits that you don't want. The process is fairly simple: examine your system for weak points and then add rules and limitations or remove effects to patch it up.

When trying to break a magic system, there are four main issues to watch out for: omnipotence, omniscience, omnipresence, and infinite wealth. If a character or the audience sees a path to any of these states, it can be a serious problem that leads to boring characters, a lack of tension, and plot holes.

Omnipotent characters possess or develop peerless or unstoppable power in their world. This can apply to any ability from controlling animals to destroying planets with their mind.

Omniscience is when a character knows everything or, at the very least, knows things they couldn't possibly know. Whether it comes from an extreme situational awareness or a surveillance network, the result is a character that can plan for anything and resolve situations before they even arise.

Then we have omnipresence. An omnipresent character is everywhere at once and in all things. They see through every mirror, hear through each gust of wind, and can appear anywhere at any time.

Lastly, there's infinite wealth. Granted, a character with endless amounts of money won't break a story like introducing a literal god will, but it's close. Advanced technology, superior training, and limitless manpower are at a character's fingertips. Even if they can't solve the conflict they're facing, they can probably pay someone who can, making any struggle trivial.

The easiest way I've found to root out these weak points is to treat the magic system as if it were real. If you had access to this magic, what would you do to get ahead in life? How would you survive and thrive in our world and in the setting of your story? If you're having a hard time thinking about it as part of real life, then imagine it's part of a video game or tabletop role-playing game. What would you do to strengthen your character and keep them alive? If you're struggling with this, you can always have someone else try to break it. If you know any power gamers or min-maxers (people who fixate on optimizing their characters in role-playing games), have them take a look.

Once identified, fixing problems with a magic system is often as easy as adding new limitations to make the elements that break your magic system impossible or at least more difficult to achieve. That said, you don't have to change anything. In fact, such "problems" can provide incredible plots, challenges, and story moments. The important thing is to be aware of what can be broken and how, and to be intentional with what gets left in the system.

Rinse and Repeat

A lot of work has been done to your magic system thus far, but this was just your first draft. You can't expect to build a perfect magic system in a single pass any more than you can expect to write the perfect story on your first try.

Now that you've gone through all the steps, you have a much better grasp of what the magic is, what it isn't, and what it needs to be. Go back to the beginning and refine it wherever you can. Brainstorm new magical effects and abilities, generate more limitations, map out more Blueprints, experiment with new themes and patterns, and recheck the alignment of the magic system with your story.

Exactly how you iterate is up to you. You can simply start at the beginning and work through the whole process again. Alternatively, you can focus on sections that feel weak or off and see if you can improve them. Don't feel you have to address all pieces equally. Some portions of the process will need more attention than others. The important thing is that you take another look. Each pass you make with any of these steps will improve your magic system.

But you don't want to iterate forever. At some point you must stop building and rebuilding and move forward with the darn thing.

But when do you stop? When is your system finished?

That's completely up to you, but there are a few simple indicators that your system might be done.

First, you've gone through the entire process. You've generated ideas, keeping only the very best. You've worked through the Blueprint and all other suggestions in this chapter. Walking through this means you have built your system with intent and covered most of the necessary aspects. That alone means more than you might think.

Second, and most importantly, it addresses all your story needs. The magic of a deep-space horror story is very different from the magic of a happy coming-of-age journey. A story and its magic system should complement, support, and enhance each other.

Finally, your magic is done when it feels done. If you've taken these steps and everything feels right, then congratulations! You just finished your magic system! Trust your gut and try not to get hung up on making things perfect.

If this was a long, frustrating experience, give yourself some time. It gets easier with time, and you now have more of the skills you need to get you there. So go forth and build some magic!

PART FIVE

Appendices

Appendix A: The Complete Blueprint

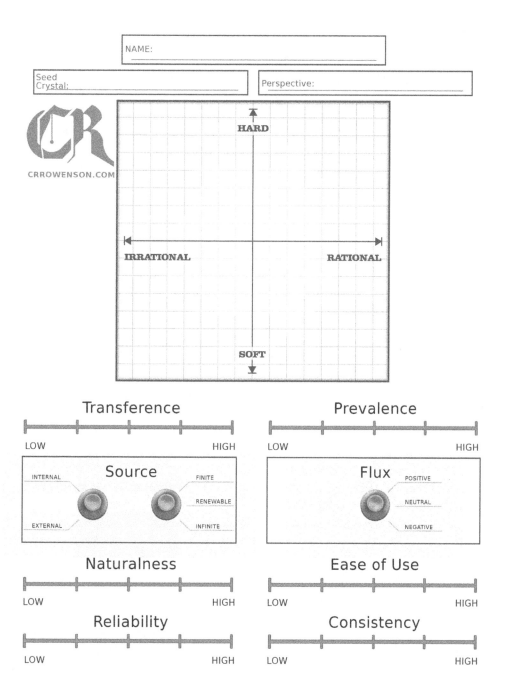

NAME:

Seed Crystal:

Perspective:

HARD

IRRATIONAL   RATIONAL

SOFT

CRROWENSON.COM

Transference

LOW   HIGH

Prevalence

LOW   HIGH

Source

INTERNAL   FINITE

                    RENEWABLE

EXTERNAL   INFINITE

Flux

            POSITIVE

            NEUTRAL

            NEGATIVE

Naturalness

LOW   HIGH

Ease of Use

LOW   HIGH

Reliability

LOW   HIGH

Consistency

LOW   HIGH

Seed Crystal

The Seed Crystal is the core concept or point of inspiration around which you will grow your entire magic system. This can be almost anything: an image, character idea, or a cool effect. Whatever it is, you want it to be short, to the point, and powerful.

Perspective

Perspective is the angle or point of view you are examining the magic system from. Different perspectives will have drastically different views of the magic system and how it works. It is important to establish this before doing any more work on the Blueprint.

Types of Magic

CRROWENSON.COM

Every magic system can be placed in one of four categories. Which category it sits in is determined by a combination of two important attributes. One indicates how well known or understood the magic is (hard / soft) and the other indicates how logical is or how much reason can be applied to its functions (rational / irrational). When combined, these two attributes illuminate which type of magic a system belongs to.

Transference

Transference is all about how the magic effects and abilities are gained, lost, loaned, or stolen from a magic-user. The more readily the power can be picked up, taken away, or shifted around, the greater the level of transference in the system.

Source

CRROWENSON.COM

The source variable examines the power within a magic system and identifies where it comes from, how much is present, and whether it can run out or be renewed. It's all about the flow of power from its original form to the production of a magical effect.

Prevalence

CRROWENSON.COM

Prevalence examines how widespread and commonplace the magic is from the chosen perspective. The more common or ubiquitous the magic is within the setting, the greater the prevalence of magic.

CR Flux

Flux is the flow rate of energy into our out of a given system. In this case, we're talking magical energy flowing into or out of the scope of the chosen perspective. If more is entering than leaving, the flux is positive. Should more energy be leaving than entering, the flux is negative. In the cases that no energy is leaving or entering, or the amount leaving equals the amount entering, the flux is neutral.

CR   Naturalness

The Naturalness variable determines how "natural" or "normal" the magic is compared to the rest of the setting around it. Systems with high naturalness feel like a smooth extension of the setting, often blending with other wondrous or strange elements until they're hard to separate from each other. Systems with low naturalness will feel like a bizarre or aberrational addition to the setting.

Ease of Use

This variable covers how easy and intuitive it is to effectively utilize the magic in a safe manner. This is yet another sliding scale ranging from extremely easy to incredibly difficult. Some magic systems require years of training, rare materials, and great personal risk to use effectively; others can be wielded with a simple thought.

Reliability

CRROWENSON.COM

Reliability indicates the extent to which the magic consistently reproduces the expected results. As with many of the other variables, this is a sliding scale from high reliability to low reliability. In a high-reliability system, a magic-user can trust the magic to perform the way they need it to, when they need it to. If a system has low-reliability the magic-user is gambling that the magic will produce the result they want.

CR

Consistency

This variable is particularly interesting and appears last on the Blueprint for a reason. Consistency looks at all the other variables and pieces of the system and indicates if and how much they deviate from the norm. It also takes into account the thematic and tonal consistency across all effects and users within the magic system. If there are a lot of exceptions and outliers in the system, this is how to account for them.

CR

Notes on:

CRROWENSON.COM

CR Effects and Abilities

These demonstrate everything the magic can do.
List every specific effect, ability, situation, achievement, or visual you can think of for the magic.

Limitations and Boundaries

These determine everything the magic cannot do.
List every capability limitation, cost, consequence, and countermeasure that exists relating to the magic.

Balance

When considering the balance of a magic system, it's best to start with a simple analysis. Examine the system for any mechanisms, loopholes, and feedback loops that might create power disparities between characters, entities, or organizations.

Perception

This considers how the magic is viewed, portrayed, or considered from a given perspective. Explore how the magic manifests, what connections it has to the character and various aspects of the worldbuilding, whether it is good or evil, whether it is desirable or not, and any opinions that might exist regarding the magic.

Glossary

Balance: Whether the magic creates power disparities between characters and in the world

Consistency: the extent to which the system can deviate from its defined settings

Ease of Use: how easy and intuitive it is to use the magic safely and effectively

Effects and Abilities: What magic-users can actually do while wielding their magic

Flux: whether Prevalence is increasing, decreasing, or remaining the same over time

Limitations and Boundaries: anything that limits the scope or use of the magic

Name: the term or terms used to reference the magic system itself

Naturalness: how natural or normal the magic is compared to the rest of the setting

Perception: the opinions and preferences related to the magic system

Perspective: the specific point of view the magic is being analyzed from

Prevalence: the abundance or absence of magic in the world

Reliability: the extent to which the magic repeatedly produces the expected results

Seed Crystal: the core concept or point of inspiration for the entire magic system

Source: where the magic comes from, how much is present, and whether it can run out

Transference: how readily the magic can be picked up, taken away, or shifted around

Types of Magic
    Hard magic: magic that is thoroughly explained and understood
    Soft magic: magic that is mysterious, hidden, and unknown
    Rational magic: can use logic to extrapolate and predict unseen portions of the system
    Nebulous magic: the details remain uncertain and cannot be extrapolated or predicted without first being shown

Appendix B: The Viral Magic System

THROUGHOUT this book we've mostly focused on well-known magic systems to serve as examples. Because I didn't make these systems, I can talk about what we see in the text or on screen only. In order to discuss motives and why you might set parts of the Blueprint certain ways, let's take a look at the Blueprint for the magic system I created: the Viral Magic System.

The Blueprint

Name

From the beginning, I knew I wanted a magic system centering on viruses, hence the immensely creative name of the Viral Magic System.

Seed Crystal

Initially, I wanted a system where characters with autoimmune deficiencies had an advantage. That quickly adapted and grew slightly into the final seed crystal for the system: magical viruses that grant special powers.

Perspective (Creator Perspective)

I usually build my magic systems before settling on characters, conflict, or even the setting. While I could have attempted to map the system from the

NAME: The Viral Magic System

Seed Crystal: Viruses that grant special powers

Perspective: Creator Perspective

CRROWENSON.COM

HARD

IRRATIONAL   RATIONAL

SOFT

Transference
LOW   HIGH

Prevalence
LOW   HIGH

Source
INTERNAL   FINITE
                  RENEWABLE
EXTERNAL   INFINITE

Flux
POSITIVE
NEUTRAL
NEGATIVE

Naturalness
LOW   HIGH

Ease of Use
LOW   HIGH

Reliability
LOW   HIGH

Consistency
LOW   HIGH

audience perspective or the universal perspective, I don't usually have enough context to do so properly. In this case, I had a basic setting and plot figured out, so I stuck the perspective that would give me the best overall comprehension of the system. That's why I always recommend starting with the creator perspective and mapping additional Blueprints afterward.

Types of Magic (Soft-Rational Magic)

I love hard-rational magic systems. I love building them, writing them, reading them, and playing them. But for this system, I pushed myself to try something new, something different. So I settled on building a soft-rational magic system.

Right away, this decision told me a few things about the system and how I needed to approach building it. To make this work, I had to leave portions of the system incomplete and viral strains unexplained to make the system feel larger and less understood. Yes, it chewed me up inside, but not identifying all the magical strains was the only way I could guarantee a soft magic system.

On top of that, the individual strains needed to feel distinct and limited to thematic connections so I could build viruses and effects that felt somewhat similar but weren't structurally oppositional or perfectly clear.

Next, for this to be a rational system, people needed the ability to anticipate and predict parts of the system or applications of the magic they hadn't seen yet. This was important to identify early on because the nature of the system actually resisted this somewhat. Each virus was going to produce its own magical effect, with little to no overlap. Without tampering, this would make magical effects of each strain feel like a discrete piece of the system.

To make this work, I had to rationalize and explain. I had to extrapolate where I could and build connections where I couldn't. Fortunately for me, that's something my twisted engineering brain is good at. So I started exploring the results and implications of the magical effects. Later in the magic-building process, I lumped the various magical effects into three distinct groups (host, vector, and environmental) and tied each group to a specific bodily fluid (sweat, blood, and digestive fluids) to build up an artificial connection between them.

This didn't all happen at once. Most of the work to make it a truly rational magic system happened after completing the Blueprint and when I was up to my eyebrows in the fine details of the system.

Transference (High)

Catching a disease isn't usually difficult. I mean, we spend most of our lives actively avoiding getting sick and it still happens. While magical in nature, the viruses spread like any other. This automatically put the Viral Magic System at a high level of transference.

But there are things that dropped it closer to medium-high transference. For one, gaining magic is fairly easy, but is it the magic you wanted? Are you catching it where and when you could actually use it? Those are other matters, both of which affect transference. On top of that, once an individual fully recovered from the illness, they were immune to further infection from that specific strain, but the viruses can mutate rapidly and infect an otherwise immune individual.

Prevalence (Medium-Low)

Increasing prevalence often increases the hardness of a magic system. Because I wanted the Viral Magic System to be a soft magic system, I knew that the prevalence needed to stay on the lower end of the spectrum. I decided that the magical viruses were quite new to the world. People knew about them even if they didn't understand what they could do. I wanted outbreaks of these magical strains to cause mayhem where they appear in the world, not treated like a common occurrence. An average person would know the viruses existed, but they would have a hard time hunting down a specific strain to infect themselves with.

Source (Infinite, Internal and External)

All magical effects come from the viruses themselves. A person can't wield magic without being infected by the virus first, and the strength of their magical effects depends on the number of virions (virus particles) present in their body. The magic is a persistent effect generated by the virions themselves and endures as long as the virions are still viable. Together, this system has an infinite, external power source, even though that external source exists inside the host's body.

Flux (Positive)

This was one of the easiest variables to lock in. The setting was normal and mundane until the strains of magical viruses started appearing in the world. That transition from no magic to any amount of magic is positive flux.

I also wanted the flux to remain positive for some time as new strains appear, spread, and mutate. With that in mind, it's pretty clear that the system has a positive flux.

Naturalness (Medium)

It was tricky getting the Viral Magic System to sit where I wanted on the scale of naturalness. I wanted something that felt more natural than unnatural, but the magical effects within the system were strange and outlandish. As unnatural as the effects feel, I structured and presented the rest of the system to drive it further up the spectrum. For one, all the effects are tied to natural bodily fluids and functions. The effects may be bizarre, but they are firmly tied to the things we know. Beyond that, the system itself pivots around viruses and how they work. Power fluctuates with the virus, creating familiar patterns and understandable circumstances.

Ease of Use (Medium-Low)

When building the Viral Magic System, I designed it to fall on the more difficult side of the spectrum. All the magical effects occurred passively, meaning there was no need for intense mental focus and direction of the effects. In that sense, the magic was automatic and easy to use, but I made it more difficult in other ways.

Mostly it came down to increasing the time required for the magic to take effect. I placed incubation periods between the moment of infection, the manifestation of powers, and the time necessary for the effects to take hold. For example, when infected with one strain, a magic-user's blood can disintegrate any inorganic matter. This breakdown process takes time, even when the virus is at the peak of its power.

In addition, I added bodily fluids as material requirements to all the effects. One strain allows teleportation but only through pools of infected blood. Another allows a character to feel and sense things remotely but only through smears of infected sweat. Blood and sweat turned out to be terrific material requirements because they were always on hand but only in limited amounts.

The last bits that factored into the ease of use for this system were experience and cleverness. No experience or education was needed to access the magic (transference). Simple exposure to the virus was enough. But once a user had the magic, experience and critical thinking were necessary to turn an odd magical phenomenon into a useful tool.

Reliability (Medium-High)

As of the writing of this book, the Viral Magic System sits somewhere around the medium-high range of the reliability spectrum. On one hand, the magic is always active. As long as the virus is present in the host, the magical effects exist and cannot be turned off. On top of that, the magic always performs the same. But while the presence and nature of the effects are uniform, their magnitude isn't.

The potency of the magic effect is entirely dependent on the number of virions within the host's body. This number will increase or decrease from day to day depending on the state of the illness within the host. And just because the magic has a certain level of strength the first time you contract the disease, that doesn't mean it will be as strong the second time. It will vary from person to person depending on their health and other conditions.

Consistency (Medium-High)

Regardless of the perspective adopted, the person infected, or the location of the individual, all the variables of the Viral Magic System are highly consistent. The powers are the same for everyone. Strength will fluctuate from person to person and with each instance of illness, but that is due to the nature of the Viral Magic System as a whole rather than an inconsistency in the variables themselves.

As for thematic and tonal consistency, the effects initially didn't feel very connected, dropping the consistency. I did my best to counteract this by strengthening the viral aspects of the system and dividing the different strains into three main groups of specific bodily fluids. Blood-borne pathogens were environmental strains. They generated magical effects that changed or impacted the setting around the magic-user. Host strains generated magical effects and changes within the user themselves and are transferred via sweat. Vector strains impacted people around the magic-user and were connected to the digestive tract: saliva, stomach fluids, urine, and feces.

Most of these tweaks came later in the building process. Initially, I just set the system on the high side of the spectrum and trusted myself to make it work in the later stages. Once finished, I think this system feels consistent in performance and theme.

Outside the Blueprint

Hopefully, the Viral Magic System has cleared up why some magic-building needs to be done outside the Blueprint. At this point, I had a solid understanding of how I wanted the system to perform and feel, but I had only a few details about what it actually did.

Magic Effects and Abilities

While creating the Viral Magic System, I went through two iterations of generating ideas. The first was general idea creation. The ideas were fairly generic and all over the place: poison cloud, technological dampening field, neural disruption zone, fire breath, poison immunity, toxic excretions, resistance to energy, fast healing, living without oxygen, body mutations, flexible bones, metal skin, and so on. But I intentionally generated more ideas than I needed in the final system so I could trim the fat and keep only the coolest options.

It wasn't until later in the building process that I hit on the idea for the different groups of effects. Once I identified them as host effects, vector effects, and environmental effects, I went through another round of brainstorming to further generate and refine my options. Here were some of the ideas I ended up with.

Environmental Effects

- » Low gravity
- » Molecular coating of objects (similar to electroplating or gold foil, but with more options)
- » Heating or cooling the surroundings
- » A neurological dampening field affecting brain functions
- » A kinetic dampening field that could be used as a shield
- » A moving cloud of darkness
- » Portals

Host Effects

» Boils filled with a powerful blistering agent
» Sweat that hardens into armor
» Blood that burns on contact with air
» A virus that removes all other viral infections from the body
» The inability to sense pain
» Enhanced muscular performance that damaged the host in the process
» Remote viewing and sensing

Vector Effects

» Mind control
» Making others unable to see, feel, or hear the host
» Transference of physical symptoms
» Rapid growth of bacterial or viral infections in others
» Slowing bodily functions of those around the host

In the end, I didn't need all these effects, so I narrowed it down to just five specific effects that I wanted to use in the story I was outlining. In the end, I settled on and further developed the Hypnosis Strain (vector strain: mind control), the Dust-Bringer Strain (environmental strain: blood can disintegrate matter), the Portal Strain (environmental strain: blood portals), the Oracle Strain (host strain: remote viewing and sensing), and the Titan Strain (host strain: enhanced muscular performance).

Balance and Magic-System Limitations

Early on, I developed a short list of rules about how the system worked, which brought their own limitations to the table and helped mostly balance the system:

1. Magical effects appear only while a person has a specific viral infection.
2. There is an incubation period between being infected and manifesting magical symptoms and powers.
3. The infection doesn't last forever. Some viral infections last only a few days.
4. Healthier individuals have their powers for less time than others.
5. Peak magical power occurs at the height of the sickness. Therefore, the most powerful effects are present only for a short window.

6. When you're sick, well . . . you feel like crap.
7. The more simultaneous infections you have, the more likely they are to kill you.
8. You can become immune to a viral strain and therefore lose access to magic.
9. Each virus behaves differently, requiring extensive knowledge to use it properly.

Then I set about stress-testing the system. I tried to find exploitable quirks, feedback cycles, and power loops. The initial nine rules covered a lot, but there were issues, particularly around the Hypnosis Strain, the Dust-Bringer Strain, and the Portal Strain. I added further restrictions. For the Hypnosis Strain, I added exposure time and delay before the target was fully affected. The Dust-Bringer Strain is now slower and affects only noncellular matter. I also tied each class of effect to a specific bodily fluid. Hosts infected with the Portal Strain could create portals only through their own blood, greatly limiting the size and frequency of the portals they could make.

There was one other balance issue across the whole system: magic-users could work together to amplify some effects. People could farm others for contagious magical fluids. But this imbalance was helpful for only a few select effects and takes so much effort to execute that I was fine leaving it in the system as it was.

Perception

Just as with any magic system, there are a wide variety of opinions and perceptions of the Viral Magic System in my story world. Most people find the viruses frightening. They are new, nobody knows where they came from, nobody knows how they work, and an outbreak of a strain causes chaos. But not everyone feels this way. There are some individuals that see the magic as a powerful tool for gaining wealth and inflicting terror on others. Some see it as a puzzle to solve and understand. While the perception can vary a great deal, most people see it as a bad and frightening thing.

And there you have it. The entire Viral Magic System mapped and explained using the Blueprint. As you can see, the Blueprint is extremely helpful when developing a holistic understanding of your magic system and how it can be tweaked and changed to fit into your story and world.

Afterward

Thank you so much for reading The Magic-System Blueprint. If you enjoyed this book or found it useful, please leave a review on the platform of your choice (Amazon, Goodreads, etc.). It really does help.

If you would like to print off a additional copies of the Blueprint, you can find PDFs of all three formats (core, essential, and deluxe) on my website. *https://crrowenson.com/magic-system-blueprint-downloadable-files/*

Should you like to learn more about magic systems, you can browse my articles and videos at *https://crrowenson.com* or sign up for my weekly newsletter at *https://crrowenson.com/newsletter-for-friends/*

Whatever you do, start building that magic system, and stay awesome!